The story
of
a watch company

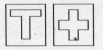

The story
of
a watch company

Estelle Fallet

SWISS WATCHES SINCE 1853

Dear friends of Tissot,

Tissot is a culture, a mentality; Tissot is a company of emotion, universally recognised for its skill in creating and producing the Swiss watch. The Swiss watch that we would all like to own because it is beautiful and of top quality, and because it is made with all the love that we feel for our watches.

«The story of a watch company», written to celebrate the 150th anniversary of the Tissot brand, will delight every buyer of a Tissot watch, in the same way as it has delighted us all at Swatch Group.

I wish you great pleasure in reading it.

Nicolas G. Hayek
Chairman of the Board of Tissot Ltd.
Chairman of the Board of The Swatch Group Ltd.

Biel/Bienne, 4th October 2002

Preface

This book is a gift offered during 2003 to everyone who buys a Tissot watch. As such, it is a symbol of the close relationship that has existed for many years between the Tissot watch company and its customers throughout the world.

The year 2003 marks the 150th anniversary of the company founded in Le Locle, Switzerland, in 1853. To mark this occasion, we have taken the opportunity of presenting a gift to our customers in the shape of a book about the company's rich, century-and-a-half-long history. We have chosen to share this history because we think that the heritage for which we have responsibility deserves to be known, not just by a limited circle of initiates, but by the public at large. We also wanted give an insight into a world often thought of as hermetic and some what secretive.

When I became President of Tissot in Spring 1996, the brand was well known and had a good reputation, and was popular with retail watch-sellers in Switzerland and abroad. Today, after six years at the helm, I know how important the historical heritage of the company is. Every day, I discover fresh facets of Tissot and its past. In order to share this wealth, I wanted to publish an impressionistic account, a kind of patchwork quilt representing the various aspects of the human and industrial activities of the company.

It is something of a gamble to publish a book on horology that will find favour with a large number of people, especially at the end of the 20th century, a century characterised by the rapid development of communications technology, including television, telex, fax, the written press and the internet. But I wanted to take on this challenge, as a kind of homage to the Tissot heritage. Instead of choosing to present the history of the Le Locle company using multimedia techniques, I wanted first for it to be recorded in black and white, on paper. Print is a medium that lasts, unlike our actions, which are isolated and ephemeral.

I have observed how the rapidity of developments in global communication has created a kind of gap separating us from the technologies used in watchmaking. The watch industry feels the need to return to its roots, to the authenticity of its values, its tradition, its *savoir-faire*. Badly shaken by the oil crisis of 1973 and the economic downturn of 1975, the watch industry of the 1990s realised that it had come close to seeing a number of ancient skills lost forever. It knows now that its survival attests to its inherent quality, and it is also conscious of the fact that continuity is essential if its marvellous heritage – constituted not only of *savoir-faire*, but also of emotional input – is to flourish.

Tissot is now in its 150th year. This anniversary affords us the opportunity of publishing a volume which is substantially different from the traditional literature on the Swiss watch industry.

That is why I wanted the book to be of the same size and have the same format and graphics as a paperback. I suggested that the author write in a style appropriate to a paperback, since this is an historical novel, whose anecdotes hold the reader in suspense and whose pace makes for a good read. Immersed in the narrative, the reader will become familiar with the Jura, the birthplace of the Swiss and French watch industries, and get to know its people and its watches. Photographs and illustrations will help to put names to faces and give an idea of the beauty of the region.

Several million copies of this book are being printed: an innovative act, typical of the long tradition of innovation of the Le Locle-based company.

The Tissot book belongs to a well defined environment, which, beyond the product itself, is concerned with strengthening the links between manufacturer and customer – public and press relations, visual presentations, packaging, a presence in retail outlets and public areas, customer service. Each sector exists to ensure that standards remain high. And each of the Tissot employees in the 150 countries in which they are the brand's ambassadors works to maintain the image and renown of the company, for which I thank all of them sincerely.

Six years ago, the word most often used to describe Tissot was «traditional». Since then, we have worked towards giving real meaning to the «plus» sign – the white cross that figures on the Swiss flag – which is part of our logo. The environment we have created is a stimulant; it encourages dynamism. For even if the connotations attached to the word «tradition» are positive, we know that, today, our clients want to associate themselves through their choice of watch with the trends, colours and materials defining our contemporary lifestyle. That is why our attention to detail and to the quality of our products is unflagging. We

12

associate «innovation» with traditional values.

We have had the opportunity of building on the foundations laid down when the SSIH Group was taken over by the Société Suisse de Microélectronique (SMH, or Swiss Microelectronics Company), placed under the direction of Nicolas G. Hayek at the beginning of the 1980s. Mr. Hayek has been the driving force behind a number of Tissot projects which have met with success all over the world. The *Rock-Watch* and the *Two Timer* are just two examples.

Tissot is the leading industrial manufacturer of traditional Swiss watches. The company stands out from the competition thanks to its complementary products, which are its strength. An example: the *T-Touch* is the synthesis of the latest technological developments realised within the Swatch Group. More than a watch, it is a piece of technical prowess, a wonder of the watchmaker's art. However, the world's most high-tech watch is, thanks to its tactile function, unequalled in its user-friendliness. As well as the *T-Touch*, Tissot's product range also features the *T-Collection*, whose watches are often avant-garde and always chime with contemporary trends. We are happy that Tissot's products, at once varied and homogeneous, have won the approval of the public.

For us, this synchronicity between respect for the past and creative innovation is of central importance. That is why I am proud to say that

13

no other traditional watch company has ever produced anything like the book you presently have in your hands. It is an authentic chronicle, at once a history of men and women and a history of industrial challenges: a history woven around living anecdotes, which have conquered the transforming effects of time.

So, without further ado, I invite you to take the time to discover this history. Let us enter the world of Tissot together. Let us push open the doors of our company ...

François Thiébaud, July 2002

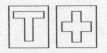

While the TGV on the Mediterranean line whisks me smoothly towards new vistas, I consult my watch.

It's not long before I see a viaduct of high-tech design. It reflects, as in a glass brightly, the famous Avignon Bridge, a truncated vestige of the past. The two images soon give way to a refined, sober, elegant station drawn in metallic lines. No slender clock tower, no pealing bells, just a gash in the wall where the hours and minutes tick by in digital figures. They are all that is required to confirm that the trains are on time.

The month of June 2002 offers itself to the first migrants of the summer. They are taking the opposite route from mine, which leads me away from the warmth of the Côte d'Azur.

On the flight, a few days earlier, to the Nice coast, the hostess graciously provides me with a glossy magazine. I turn its pages distractedly. My attention is captured by an advert, which announces:

«Tissot. Swiss watches since 1853».

There are values, which go beyond time, like attention to details and a continuous quest for innovation, both technological and aesthetic. Values which, combined with traditional Swiss watchmaking, ensure that Tissot always remains avant-garde – since 1853.

My eyes are riveted to the words; it's probably because I'm bound for Switzerland, which is, I've heard, a paradise for tourists, chocolate, banks and watches. What shall I discover beyond the lakes and the mountains sprinkled with snow that the seductive images of the photographers have made famous throughout the world?

Tissot *T-Win*, 2002.

The twin-dial Tissot watch has a smooth line. Its name, «T-Win», calls to mind that of the manufacturer. A slogan subtly underlines the importance accorded to technology: «Tissot. Innovators by tradition …». Two dates are underlined: 1853–2003.

Tissot pocket watch,
Revue internationale de l'horlogerie, 1923.

I find it difficult to imagine what a watch might have represented in the 19th century; my grandfather himself only ever had a single wristwatch, an austerely square, archaic-looking thing. But the theatre, with its solid middle-class citizens solemnly pulling out their round fob watches hanging from golden chains, has given me an insight into the past.

«Since 1853…». How does a brand survive across the generations? The 19th century seems such a long time ago. Personally, I'm an aficionado of fashion and its shifting choices; I appreciate changing styles and am not averse to challenging habit, always ready to criticise the ponderous monotony of traditions whose authentic character escapes me.

I change my watch frequently, depending on what I wear, on how I'm feeling too, depending, of course, on what I'm doing ... but I nevertheless have the vague impression that a watch is an object linked to emotion – the emotion of the instant (like an unexpected gift); the emotion of the object (able to instil a particular sentimental attachment); the emotion of time (which passes, never to return). ... The watch as time-keeper? The watch as functional object? I don't think it is true of me personally, but I have the feeling that the object on my wrist is perpetuating a tradition, time-honoured skills, even a mentality, the sources of which are unknown to me. The train comes to a halt.

At the Gare de Lyon, a lady sits down near my numbered seat. Jovially, she asks how my journey's going. She's from Toulon, she explains, a city whose walls have been warmed by the rays of the sun for weeks now. Madame is travelling to the Jura to enjoy the freshness of the region's pine forests. Her lilting accent is characteristic of the south of France; her bracelets accompany her gestures and the clear, tinkling chatter of her voice.

My travelling companion is resting now, her brown hands becalmed on her lap. Around her wrist is a fine gold bracelet; at its centre, a watch dial and two slender hands. I lean forward to see what make it is – «Tissot»!

She looks at me, smiling, while I, a little embarrassed, compliment her on her choice of wristwatch. She tells me that her children gave it to her for one of her birthdays, her fiftieth to be precise, she says, slightly flustered.

A Tissot shop window, circa 1965.

It's a Swiss watch. A lovely present. I've only had to take it to a retailer in Geneva once, to change the battery. But, you know, Tissot also make mechanical watches.

Noticing my perplexity, she continues, *Watches with mechanical movements, masterpieces of miniaturisation, in which each wheel, each gear, each pinion plays a precisely defined role.*

I don't know much about it, but my maternal grandfather in the French Jura worked for a watch company. He showed me his tools and explained how watches worked. What fascinated me most about him were his calmness and skill, and the delicacy of the tiny pieces he laid out in front of him: balance wheels, hairsprings, screws, wheels of all sizes … every piece, he said, fits into the elegantly designed calibres characteristic of each manufactory. It seems that these days the tools of the watchmaker have been replaced by large, efficient machines.

We arrive in Geneva. It is time to take our leave and to wish each other all the best for the future.

She turns and says: «*Why don't you spend some time in Geneva, its shops are full of the treasures of Swiss watchmaking. And don't forget … Rue du Mont-Blanc – Tissot!*»

Swiss watchmaking … my pleasure trip takes an unexpected turn. I already know that the adventure of the watchmaker's art and the history of time will meld together to render my journey an unforgettable one.

What surprises does Switzerland hold in store for me?

At the heart of the Old Continent, at the heart of Europe, Switzerland seems like an island. People say that life is good there, even if, at various moments in its history, the country has not been spared economic crises, unemployment and social unrest. A peacefully, politically neutral island, attached to its democratic traditions and to its ancient federalism. After all, isn't this the homeland of William Tell, the sanctuary of myriad refugees, the true

confederation of pluralism and diversity? Four official languages are spoken here, each of them inscribed in the Federal Constitution, which is conserved in Berne, the country's capital. German Switzerland, French-speaking Switzerland, Grisons and the Ticino are, in spite of a few nuances in terms of cultural sensibility, entities united in a single whole.

Switzerland applied to become part of the United Nations in 2002, just before my visit. However, despite the fact that the country has taken its time in joining the club, it has always played an active role backstage. Switzerland is quick to defend the rights of man, civility and justice around the world. And, in the light of events and ongoing legal affairs, it is ready to recognise its mistakes and does not balk at reviewing its history.

You can travel across this small territory in just a few hours. To the north lies Germany, to the south, Italy; to the west, France, and to the east, Austria. It's a country on a human scale, full of contrasting landscapes, of modern cities and of flower-laden farms.

What will I learn here in Switzerland of the country's prestigious industry?

In my magazine, I find the corporate names of several different watch firms, each one accompanied by the same phrase: «A Swatch

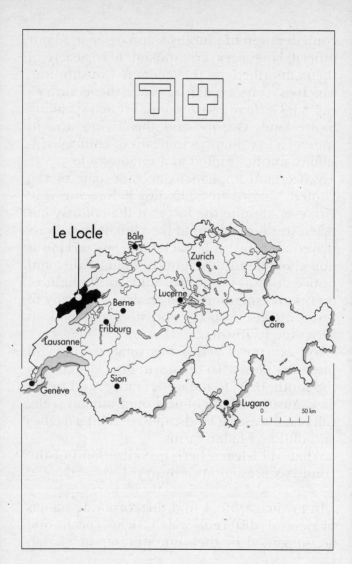

Le Locle

Bâle

Zurich

Berne

Lucerne

Fribourg

Coire

Lausanne

Sion

Genève

Lugano

0   50 km

Group company». While I'm already familiar with the reasonably priced, fun watch that first appeared in the early 1980s, a watch whose look, technology, price and packaging revolutionised the industry, and while I've already visited Swatch's spruce outlets the world over, it is only now – transfixed before my screen in a cyber-café in the city of John Calvin (austere Geneva!) – that I appreciate the sheer size of the Swatch Group.

Nicolas G. Hayek, President, Chairman of the Board and Chief Executive Officer, defines the philosophy of Switzerland's largest watch group:

The Swatch Group has a very special emotional culture. We produce beauty, sensuality, emotionality in watches – and we also produce high-tech on your wrists. Both, emotionality or poetry and high-tech, are part of what we feel towards our customers. We love them genuinely. We want them to be happy – we want YOU to be happy!

Welcome!

Who is this smiling president, whose website features a watch indicating – in quasi-esoteric signs – @633.beats?

Nicolas G. Hayek (founder and president of Hayek Engineering SA, which is active the world over) has played a decisive role in the expansion of the Swatch Group by constantly breathing his energy into a host of extraordinary projects, including the strategic decision to launch the Swatch; the development of the brands Omega, Longines, Rado, Tissot in the 1980s and Breguet and Glashütte in 1999 and 2000 respectively; the capture of the title of World No. 1 in the watch sector; and the rescue of the entire Swiss watch industry, which was so sorely tried after the major crisis of 1975–1981, by providing watch parts to all its sales representatives. Numerous new jobs have been created, and as many jobs and production centres saved, thanks to Mr. Hayek, who, in recognition of his services, has received honorary degrees from the Universities of Neuchâtel and Bologna.

I also discover that the consulting company founded by Nicolas Hayek has been active since 1963 in both the private and public sectors; I learn that Mr. Hayek played a leading role in the 1983 merger between the holding companies ASUAG *Allgemeine Schweizerische Uhrenindustrie Aktiengesellschaft* and SSIH the *Société Suisse pour l'Industrie Horlogère*, or Swiss Society for the Horology Industry, which became SMH *Société Suisse de Microélectronique*, or Swiss Microelectronics Company, and then, in 1998, The Swatch Group.

Nicolas G. Hayek.

If the federal authorities have chosen Nicholas G. Hayek to conduct a study on the national exhibition – Expo02 – whose promising content I am happy to discover, it is because of the clear-sightedness and rigour of the advice offered by the overall head of the Swatch Group. Indeed, his opinions are well respected both in Switzerland and abroad, especially when German and French governments solicit his expert advice.

Consequently, the Swatch Group's figures are impressive: *Some 50 nations, about 70 languages, over 440 reporting units, almost 20,000 collaborators. In the year 2000 sales exceeded the CHF 4 billion mark for the first time.*

In 2002, the group, as a manufacturer and retailer of finished watches, is made up of the following brands: Breguet, Blancpain, Léon Hatot, Jaquet Droz, Glashütte, Omega for the prestige and luxury sector; Longines and Rado in the top-of-the-range sector; Tissot, Calvin Klein, Union, Certina, Mido, Hamilton in the mid-range sector; and Swatch and Flik Flak in the basic sector. Endura produces «private label» watches for certain consumers.

Judging by the size of the industrial group, reinforced by its pyramid structure, I am not surprised to discover further that it is active in microelectronics, micromechanics, telecommunications and the automotive industry. The Swatch Group has been designated as official partner of the IOC for time-keeping and displaying results at the 28th Olympic Games, to be held in Athens in 2004, at the 20th Winter Olympics in Turin in 2006, and at the 2008 Olympics and the 2010 Winter Olympics.

Tissot *PR 100*, 1984.

It's true, I said to myself as a lover of sporting events, *the Swatch Group has always been, with a few exceptions, the official time-keeper of almost all the Olympic Games of the 20th century. And, if memory serves, I believe that it is the Tissot PR100 watch that was selected as official time-keeper by the Austrian, German and Swiss teams in 1984.*

I observe once again that the head offices and production centres of all the brands of the Swatch Group are concentrated in the region referred to as the Jurassian Arc – from Geneva to Bienne to Schaffhausen and Basel. It is in this last-named city, famous for its association with the scholar Erasmus, that a World Watch and Jewellery Fair is held every year; the trade papers that I have delivered to my home describe it at length, providing numerous illustrations.

Here is the precise itinerary that I wish to follow – first from Geneva to Neuchâtel to visit the famous Tissot watch manufactory, which had come to my attention by chance and which, I learn, is situated at Le Locle in the canton of Neuchâtel.

Thenceforth, I start to collect detailed and general information. I reach for a notebook and sketch out a genealogy – Swatch Group (1998), which descends from SMH (1983–1985), itself a descendant of SSIH–ASUAG (1983), SSIH being the result of the association between Omega and Tissot in 1930.

I have my Ariadne's thread! But I still have to concentrate on following it!

Encouraged by his polite and deferential attitude, I question the Geneva salesman seated behind his counter.

How long has watchmaking been a feature of the region?

I can tell you that if a Genevan or Jurassian watchmaker who worked with files and engraver's burins in the 1650s came back to this part of the country, he would recognise nothing of his surroundings or his tools; he would recognise nothing of the ambience and atmosphere in which he lived, for the watchmaking industry has undergone prodigious changes. The art of watchmaking is an exceptional one, rich in discoveries, rich in experiences, and rich in talent!

But where does this art originate?

Minouvis. A Jura watchmaker's workshop.
Collection MIH (La Chaux-de-Fonds, Suisse).

Watchmaking has no single birthplace, in the sense of its first craftsmen coming from a specific location, for the great names associated with the main discoveries through which chronometry was able to advance are French, English, Dutch, German and Italian. The problem of the division of time and of its measurement is universal and has been posed in all epochs... my interlocutor concludes sententiously, while a customer interrupts our conversation by placing his watch on the counter; he wants a link removed from the steel strap of his Tissot Atollo.

Back on the street, I consider the salesman's phrases, at once laconic and pregnant with meaning; I would have loved to chat for longer, to find out more! While waiting for the exact time of my departure indicated by the clock at the coach station, I put my ideas in order; I am going to Neuchâtel in several stages, the rhythm of the journey dictated by the Post Office coach's stopping-off places.

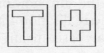

My thoughts wander as I am lulled by the muffled purr of the engine.

Grown-up people often say that you should not waste time. They also say that you must be on time and look at their watches and clocks with a knowing air. For the child that I was, these solemn words had little meaning; I was still trying to tell the difference between yesterday, today and tomorrow, Sunday and Monday, workdays and holidays … the nuances of temporal perception only came to life for me when, on leaving the magical spectacle of a circus, I blurted out in surprise, *It's already over! How quickly time passes!*

There is a time to work, a time to rest and sleep, to eat, to travel and to enjoy oneself. Men have learned to measure time ever more accurately, the better to organise their activities. Our distant ancestors noted how the moon replaced the sun, how one season followed another; the realisation that night follows day on a regular basis meant that they were able to break time down into months, hours, minutes and seconds.

Large-volume timepiece,
The Land of Micro-Precision, Tissot, 1953.

At the third stroke, it will be thirteen hundred hours, three minutes and forty seconds ...

Our forebears illustrated the ages of Man, from childhood to youth to adulthood to old age. By expressing this immutable reality, identical for all, they invented instruments to measure the passage of time – simple sticks or obelisks, clepsydras or hourglasses, solar dials, calendars and clocks.

Vague memories of primary school. The teacher explains, *More than five hundred years ago, men made the first clocks using a complicated system of toothed wheels operated by weights.* Tick tock, tick tock ... Obsessed with mechanics and science, men eventually managed to create watches which had no tick tock at all! Ecstatically I realised, *My plastic watch produces only a muffled sound which goes 'tock, tock, tock' ...*

The road taken by the Post Office coach in which I am sitting winds along the shore of a lake and then around the feet of vineyard-strewn hills and dark mountains. On the opposite horizon, tall silhouettes cut through the sky.

Look at that magnificent view of the Alps! the driver says to me. *Do you know the region?*

When I tell him I don't, but that I would like to know more about the local watchmaking industry, he embarks upon a picturesque story.

I am Combier … so I know a thing or two about watchmaking. My father was master of escapements at the School of Watchmaking at the Sentier. When the factories in the Joux Valley closed in the crisis, I joined the Post Office … I swapped uniforms, you know!

The watchmakers of Geneva taught us the trade. Not us, personally, I mean! It was a very long time ago, as you can imagine! It was around the middle of the 17th century. They spread out over the whole of the Vaud canton, occupying the shores of Lake Léman as far as Yverdon. From there to Neuchâtel and La Neuveville, and later to the Jura Mountains, which form the frontier with France. You see those mountain crests we're following? We're taking the same journey as our distant forebears … weighed down by their trunks and their slow horses. Just imagine that!

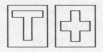

At Neuchâtel, I get out at the foot of Castle Hill, the seat of the Government, as my guide-book tells me. Neuchâtel was once a principality, ruled over at one time or another by Marie de Nemours, the Kings of Prussia and, fleetingly, Marshal Berthier, the faithful ally of Napoleon I. Neuchâtel became a Swiss canton on 12th September 1814. The tiny country proclaimed itself a Republic on 1st March 1848, while across Europe the royalist yoke was being shaken.

Inhabitants of Le Locle,
A pacific revolution has just taken
place in our locality.
Civil and military authority
has recently been placed in our hands.
We immediately put it to use
by recommending calm and order,

which, if need be, we shall impose.
This is our programme:
A forgetting of the past;
The respect of people and property;
Order based on liberty.

The Committee
Henry Grandjean, David Perret fils, Auguste
Lambelet,
Auguste Leuba, Edouard Girod

Look! The role of the Neuchâtel watchmakers – the ones who came down from the mountains to capture the Castle – is highlighted in this relatively bloodless revolutionary episode!

Castle Hill, Neuchâtel.

On the façade of the Collegiate Church, from where the reformer Guillaume Farel harangued the crowds, I can make out the partial design of a watch dial.

It's time to find out where I'll be staying while I'm here.

The visitor's guide to the Castle explains that while the territory of Neuchâtel covers little more than 800 square kilometres, divided into six districts, the variety of its landscapes is as surprising as the charm of its features. Is it not true that an officer of the French Guards visiting the Pays de Neuchâtel in 1789 wondered whether there could really be a place as singular and as agreeable to explore in the whole world? Did not the poet Lamartine, awestruck by the largest entirely Swiss lake, contemplate it endlessly, comparing it to the vast reaches of the Jura's pastures, a *thick wall of mountains sloping gently down to France?*

Oh time, suspend thy flight! And your propitious hours,
Suspend your course!
Let us savour these fleeting pleasures
Of the most beautiful of our days!
[Alphonse de Lamartine, The Lake, 1849]

The heavy door of the Museum of Art creaks opens mysteriously. I slip through the gap and stand at the foot of a monumental staircase.

I am at first astonished and then absorbed by an immense triptych. I let my gaze wander through Paul Robert's vast allegory of «L'industrie»: the tormented age which gave birth to the modern industrial world … the fascination exerted by money. A watch factory in La Chaux-de-Fonds; a locomotive makes a surrealistic appearance amidst the dangerously excited figures of the composition. Industry is accused of being the cause of this staggering disorder. A few placid men and women escape the clutches of this new-born power … assiduous watchmakers.

Allegories of the dangers of modern times … The year is 1890. Rebellious proletarians, bourgeois blinded by greed, the new disorder. All is stigmatised.

The artist invites us to preserve the traditions of the past.

At the Tourist Office, I start to tap away again at a computer keyboard; need I mention that, as well as poetry, I appreciate the speed of modern information media?

The Pays de Neuchâtel website opens with a title and some figures: *Watchmaking, products and brands.* I have the impression that my curiosity is about to be satisfied by a number of new elements. All the more so in that I have noticed at the corner of the street a shop display featuring a Tissot product.

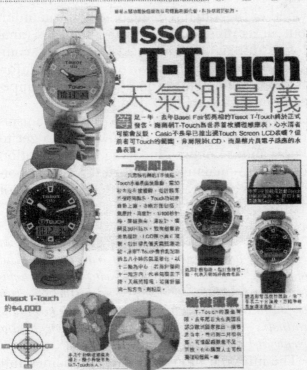

T-Touch in China, 2002.

Called the «*T-Touch* ? - The touch-screen watch» and ringed with a brightly coloured, apple-green sticker, this new high-tech product is a multi-functional electronic watch whose tactile screen reacts to the touch of a finger. The ticket on the strap details not only whether the watch is made of steel or titanium, but all its functions too: hours, minutes (analogue display), seconds (LCD display), compass with analogue display, date, weather information, altimeter, chrono, alarm and temperature gauge with LCD display.

But how can I find the fragile mechanisms that I've been told about, how am I to get to know about fine watchmaking, the reputation of which – making light of international borders – has encouraged me to define the goal of my journey?

For three hundred years, the watchmakers of Neuchâtel have accumulated an irreplaceable fund of experience. The qualities of Neuchâtel watchmaking – innovation, technology and aesthetics – can be found in all the activities and fields linked to the industry and contribute to the renown of the Neuchâtel name in world markets.

The infra-red mouse conjures up names and dates. I memorise two of them, both of which are already familiar to me: Ferdinand Berthoud, Watchmaker to the Navy of the King of France; and Abraham-Louis Breguet, founder of a renowned family firm which has remained intact since the middle of the 18th century.

From Placemont sur Couvet and Neuchâtel respectively, these two watchmakers illustrate the fine reputation enjoyed by the canton in foreign climes.

And just to think that now, thanks to a twice daily TGV train link, Neuchâtel is less than four hours from Paris!

A Neuchâtel farm.

Yet other names appear, certain of which – originating in Neuchâtel – I saw in the display window of the local watch retailer: the founding fathers Daniel JeanRichard and Abraham-Louis Perrelet, creator of a self-winding watch, the forerunner of today's automatic watches; the scientists Jacques-Frédéric Houriet, Sylvain Mairet and Phinée Perret; the clockmakers Samuel Roy and Aimé Billon; Henri-Louis Jaquet Droz, the clockmaker-mechanic whose famous musical automata were displayed throughout the Kingdom of Spain; Philippe DuBois, Frédéric-Louis Favre-Bulle; Edouard Bovet, called Bovet of China; Henri Grandjean, who set up a branch of his Le Locle-based company in Brazil; Jules Jürgensen and Ulysse Nardin whose marine chronometers sail the world's oceans; Pierre-Frédéric Ingold, a forerunner in the field of mechanical technology; Paul Ditisheim, maker of precision chronometers; Paul Buhré, Henry Moser and Charles-Emile Tissot, whose watches were to be found in the deepest recesses of the Empire of All the Russias! It is remarkable, but nevertheless true, that most of these watchmakers practised their art in Le Locle.

Listen, why don't I share the following anecdotes with you?

I shall write them in italics, so that you know that I have read them and not made them up.

Sylvain Mairet, the old artisan born in 1805, was the perfect example of the artist watchmaker. After discovering a number of plates that had been polished so badly that they were ruined, an indignant Mairet apostrophised the guilty parties in the following, searing terms 'You people should be shot!' The incident had no disagreeable ramifications, for Sylvain Mairet was a good man at heart and incapable, as they say, of hurting a fly.

A very beautiful young woman, wearing a lofty «Frégate» wig and a blue and pink panniered, hoopframe dress, was seated at the harpsichord, smiling, her breast somewhat oppressed as if by a sudden emotion. She looked to the right, to the left, then her fingers ran back and forth across the keyboard, tapping out a gavotte.

The gavotte was followed by a minuet, then by a fantasia, which was at first lively, then languorous, and finally more ... and ... more ... s a d.

When she had finished, the young woman made a bow and, taking a rose from a fine crystal vase, breathed in its perfume and became perfectly immobile ... a gracious android. Pierre Jacquet, this is your masterpiece!

I also discover that the Nobel Prize was awarded in 1920 to Charles-Edouard Guillaume, of Fleurier, for his research on the metals used in horology. I really am in a part of the world rich in learned men!

In 1967, it was a Neuchâtel research establishment, the Electronic Horology Centre, that designed and produced the first quartz wristwatches, obliterating contemporary world records for precision. In 2002, the Astronomic and Chronometric Observatory of Neuchâtel participated in the development of caesium atomic clocks whose unequalled accuracy conferred on them the honour of taking part in the European space program.

Thus, Neuchâtel horology covers all the technical and productive aspects of its industry; it develops and refines equipment used in the production of mechanical components for watches (*ébauches*, escapements, jewels, springs, hairsprings, dials, hands, etc.) and electronic components (integrated circuits, micromotors, batteries, quartz resonators, displays, and so on). It organises and carries out the production of cases and dials in the local area.

But who is behind Neuchâtel horology? How am I going to get close to its enterprise, its executives, its projects, how am I going to get to know its products?

Why not go up to Le Locle, the «Mother commune», my young hostess at the Tourist Office suggests, handing me a map of the area. *You'll be able to see the museums and factories. At La Chaux-de-Fonds, they even explain how to read the history of horology in the walls of the town and its outskirts. ... Follow the 'Bon pied, bon œil' guide, and watch out, those guys are great practical jokers!*

Say no more, Mademoiselle! I shall leave Neuchâtel after visiting «ArtePlage», which, in the summer of 2002, is hosting a section of the National Exhibition, which is providing an original, aesthetic and festive image of what Switzerland is today, behind the flags and the geraniums.

I would happily live in this round Palace Balance made all of wood, I say to myself wistfully on my way out.

The Pavilion Balance, Expo 02, Neuchâtel.

On my way up to Le Locle, on the slopes of the mountain, I notice the Neuchâtel region's most amazing geological landmark: an immense circle of boulders known as the Creux-du-Van.

I've not seen its like anywhere during the course of my extensive peregrinations.

Apparently you need a head for heights to venture near the edge of the impressive cliffs. It is only thanks to a lucky detour that I had the pleasure of enjoying cheese fondue with country bread along with a glass of robust white wine and a delicious kirsch.

I will say nothing of my laborious trek down the mountain across woods which were maliciously hostile to my progress!

La Chaux-de-Fonds: arrival at 9.48 p.m. precisely.

The Creux-du-Van.

I put off my visit to the «Watchmaker's Metropolis» till tomorrow; but I nevertheless admire, under the station's portico, the vast fresco representing the working men and women of the local watchmaking industry, rendered immobile and serene by the vigorous, solid strokes of the artist who put his name to the work in 1951 – Georges Dessoulavy.

Nestling 1,000 metres (3,000 feet) up in the mountains, La Chaux-de-Fonds is the highest town in Europe. The night air is perfect – calm and refreshing.

G. Dessoulavy.
Fresco in La Chaux-de-Fonds railway station, 1951.

La Chaux-de-Fonds, birthplace of the romantic painter Léopold Robert, of the architect Charles-Edouard Jeanneret, better known as Le Corbusier, of the writer Blaise Cendrars, and of the car manufacturer Louis Chevrolet, is Switzerland's most representative 19th century new town. This fertile breeding ground of the Art Nouveau movement is arranged in a series of steep streets set out in a grid. On certain of these streets I stop in front of the ghosts of signs painted on the façades – Paul Ditisheim Watches Solvil, Movado, Breitling watches, Eberhardt Chronometers. The harmonious modern factories of Corum and Ebel bear witness to the inspiration of contemporary architects. These architects are not unaware of the fact that the town's School of Art flew the flag for the artistic currents of the early 20th century: Villa Marguerite and Villa Turque also attest to the success of a certain local watchmaking industrialist.

The International Museum of Horology (MIH),
La Chaux-de-Fonds.

This morning, I have spent a couple of fascinating hours at the International Museum of Horology, which is itself a masterpiece of troglodytic architecture, built in the 1970s. I slowly allow myself to become absorbed in the world's long tradition of time-keeping.

The Watchmaker's Metropolis is giving up its secrets. It was in the 19th century that it acquired its title, thanks to the extent of its industry and the number of its workshops, its *établissage* centre and its watch factories.

The Museum's curator, a small, round, very welcoming little chap, points out, with an air of importance, that the caricature of Numa the Optimist, *famous for his jolly aspect and the* migros *slap bang in the middle of his forehead*, as well as the *no less famous* figure of Ouin Ouin,

H. Guinand, *Numa the Optimist*,
La Chaux-de-Fonds, 1943.

Ouin Ouin, par E. Piroué,
Coll. Musée international d'horlogerie.

the fantastical engraver whose fame has spread beyond the confines of French-speaking Switzerland, were both born in Le Locle.

You mean you don't know the character? I'll tell you a funny story!

After a long escapade, Ouin Ouin turns up at the workshop one Friday to collect his wages. The boss, who has had it up to his eyeballs with the waster, calls him in to the office.

- *Ouin Ouin, this time you've gone beyond the pale, I've had enough of you, you're always messing around, you take the other workers' minds off their jobs, so here are the three days' pay I owe you …*

- *But, sir …*

- *There's no point arguing, Ouin Ouin, I've already warned you fifty times. Collect your things and get out!*

Ouin Ouin skulks away to gather his pliers and burins, folds his smock away and trudges melancholically down the stairs; when he reaches the exit he sighs despondently and thinks about how difficult it will be to find another job and about how many hoops he will have to jump through before collecting any more wages. It's heartbreaking. But, undeterred, he makes a snap decision, climbs back up the stairs, goes back into the waiting room he's just left and knocks at the boss's door.

The boss, who has only just calmed down, is hardly overjoyed.

- *I can't believe it, you again!*

Ouin Ouin doesn't let him finish. Cap in hand and ever so humbly, he asks:

- *Pardon, sir, I've heard that you've just sacked a worker and I was wondering if I might be the very man for the job ...*

In the Museum's modern section, curious eyes are drawn to the brilliant glimmer of contemporary timepieces. Naturally, I make a beeline for the Tissot watches. I discover to my surprise a number of pocket watches and pieces with leather straps which remind me of my grandfather's watch!

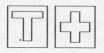

On the outskirts of the town, nicknamed the «Watchmaking Metropolis», a small aircraft with a bright livery followed by another plane sporting Tissot's colours comes to a halt beside the pastures with their grazing cows and sheep.

On the other side of the road, the shining glass of an «Advanced Watch Manufactory» Cartier attracts the gaze of the passenger of the strange blue and white shuttle travelling towards Besançon and onwards beyond Dijon to Paris and London.

Just a few miles and a mere seven minutes away from La Chaux-de-Fonds, I arrive in Le Locle: another watchmaking town, nicknamed the «City of Precision», probably because the School of Engineers of the Canton of Neuchâtel is based there and the Technical College has its horology department there.

Welcome to the region of Horology and Microtechnology.

A stone's throw from the Franco-Swiss border, deep in the limestone rock, the subterranean windmills of the Col des Roches are, as the poster in the entrance of the prettily decorated little station obligingly informs me, a unique attraction in Europe. In fact, I can't wait to descend into these cool caverns to meditate gently on the passage of time, on life's temporal aspects, on the evolution of the machine age, and on the development of microtechnology.

Achieving the atemporal …

1965 construction project,
Tissot's North Tower.

Opposite the station, whose walls hum with the chaotic echoes of a nearby brass band, I see a vast white façade – the Tissot factory dominates the little town. I'm already impatient: *What will I find behind the façade? What surprises await me?*

Patience and slow-moving time…

On the terrace of the «Jet d'Eau», opposite the strange, cracked mountain through which France can be glimpsed on the horizon, I enjoy a country breakfast.

People tell pretty stories about Le Locle, I say to myself, recalling my visit to the windmills; what an invention, this «Mother Commune» of the communities established in the 16th century in the emancipated domains of La Sagne, La Chaux-de-Fonds, La Chaux des Tallières, La Brévine and Les Brenets. The local people undertook astonishing projects – clearing the forests, draining the great swamps of the valley, and even cleaving a road through the Col des Roches. How harsh life must have been for the men and women of that long-gone era.

I leaf through a soft leather-bound book.

Charming legends are recounted in the prettily bound volumes pointed out to me by the man in the bookshop near the Vieux Moutier. *Neuchâtel was an important centre for French and foreign publishing in the 18th century. You will find rare editions of the Faucher Printing House of Neuchâtel here, as well as high-quality engravings by the Girardets of Le Locle … The great Jean-Jacques Rousseau stayed in our region, as you can see from his letters.*

The bookseller has given me a good price on several old volumes. At my leisure I can gently delve into the wondrous stories – and submerge myself in the atmosphere of the watchmaker's art. My eyes run over the laid paper. These are lines full of truth.

Le Locle, late 18ᵗʰ century.

The next day we left very early for Le Locle, which is three leagues from La Chaux-de-Fonds, but there were so many houses scattered along the road that one village seemed to meld into the next. Industry and commerce are the same in these two places; in La Chaux-de-Fonds people work more on clocks, in Le Locle, on watches.

The valley in which the first town is situated is wider and better cultivated. The houses of Le Locle are more beautiful and the inhabitants even wealthier: it is difficult to get over one's surprise at seeing, in these far-flung mountains, houses that would be considered beautiful in Paris.

Horology is the largest branch of commerce; the scattered cabins in the other valleys are filled with workers employed in the first stages of watchmaking. It is in Le Locle and La Chaux-de-Fonds that watches are finished and perfected; there one finds the engravers, the gilders, the enamellers, the painters, even the inventors, for it is rare that a year goes by when they do not create new tools and mechanical instruments to improve their art.

[Pierre de Zurich, *The Swiss Journeys of Madame de La Briche in 1785 and 1788*, Attinger, undated.]

Did not Madame de La Briche take away with her a pretty enamelled châtelaine watch embellished with fine pearls and glittering with the fire of rose-cut diamonds?

Another woman of the world followed in her footsteps, using her graceful pen to recount new episodes.

I was on my way, without a rendez-vous, to visit an engine-turner whose skills are celebrated. He welcomed me amiably and politely into his workshop, where he was using an artistic instrument he had made himself to turn a few very beautifully designed

Late 18ᵗʰ-century façade in Le Locle.

watches. Behind him there was a small collection of books. I drew nearer and saw to my astonishment Rollet's «Physics», the poems of Haller translated into French, Bonnet's work on nature, a hefty tome on agriculture by the Abbé Rozier, etc. He modestly affirmed that I would find nothing worthy of my attention, for he had enjoyed no other education than the one he had given himself.

[Anna H. von Krock, *Briefe einer reisenden Dame aus der Schweiz*, 1786, Frankfurt /Leipzig, 1787.]

Will I be the faithful chronicler of my sojourn in Le Locle like the ladies of letters in the Age of Enlightenment?

Alas! My camera lets me down at the very moment I need it most! I have stopped in front of a tall red brick chimney.

Hey, Mister! Do you know why there are such big factories in our little town, which, on 31st May 2002, had precisely 10,462 inhabitants? It's because there's a world between the watch of 1681, Daniel JeanRichard's watch with its gut cord and its tin dial, and the masterpieces of the present day!

If you're working on a piece, you should go up and take some photographs of the house Le Corbu built for the industrialist Favre-Jacot, the founder of the Billodes … Zenith watches, you know!

The postman has made his delivery.

But who is Daniel JeanRichard?

I have seen a plaque with his name on it, pointing to a street in the middle of which there is a dark bronze statue erected in honour of a man wrapped in a heavy blacksmith's apron.

I need to pay a visit to the Town Library to find the clues which will lead me to a satisfactory answer.

Writing is such a precious thing! I am minded to apply myself to my own from now on ...

Daniel JeanRichard, known as Bressel, who died in 1741, is the archetypal watchmaker of the Neuchâtel Mountains. He incarnates the very notion of «horology». The statue put up in his memory in Le Locle in 1888 was designed to illustrate the fundamental values characterising the life of the «founding father» of the Neuchâtel watch industry. I find a description in the local almanac, the *Messager Boiteux* (The Limping Messenger) of 1890.

Daniel JeanRichard is depicted examining a watch belonging to Peter the Horse Trader; his intelligent head is slightly inclined towards the object, which he has never seen before. The initial instant of surprise has passed and he has begun to give it his full attention; the young man is absorbed, fascinated even, and keeping his eyes on the enigmatic piece whose

Daniel JeanRichard by Charles Iguel, Le Locle, 1888.

Monot illustrated guide, Le Locle, circa 1920.

mysteries he would like to unravel, he takes a pincer from the anvil with his right hand so that he can touch, gingerly, the watch's mechanism...

My neighbour in the silent reading room explains that he too is interested in the history of horology, and particularly in calendars. A well-informed bibliophile, he has some ideas of his own about JeanRichard. He wastes no time in providing me with a clear and precise description of those ideas.

This man, he says, «happens to be the first horological entrepreneur, in the modern sense of the term.
- *He created a product, developed from obsolete French models.*
- *He fixed a sale price adapted to the possibilities of the market.*
- *He used the retail network already set up by the lace weavers for their own products.*
- *He trained apprentices, the first of whom came from La Neuveville.*
- *He encouraged professional ties with mechanics and watchmakers specialising in equipment, tools and various supplies.*
- *He sought and purchased products not available locally, such as springs and hairsprings, from as far afield as Geneva.*
- *By selling land, he set up a fund so that he could pay his creditors before receiving payment from debtors for the sale of his goods.*

The man falls silent. He goes back to his reading, leafing through an attractive-looking Monot guide to Le Locle decorated in Art Nouveau style.

But, I ask myself, how is it that a delicate and complex activity such as watchmaking came to be practised in such an inhospitable place, with little in the way of infrastructure and far from the centres of trade?

I am surprised to find a redundant «climatic» explanation of the origins of Neuchâtel horology, an explanation based on a relationship with snow which is deeply felt in the region. This relationship is marked by a strong sense of symbolism (the immaculate era of the gestation period of the industry), filling the gaps of a declining historical memory, which has lost sight of the precise origins of the local industry.

Surrounded by snow six months of the year, the Neuchâtel mountain dweller has become industrious out of necessity. Always seated and always working, he thinks only of accelerating, dividing and multiplying his work tasks. Lively and ingenious, he pursues all possible improvements and inventions. Active and enterprising, he never stops looking for new, more distant markets for the precious and delicate products of his industry, admirable works of art in which, often unbeknownst to him, advanced science has guided his hand. The whole world over,

his watches tell the hours of the day and the night,
beating out the measure of time.
[F.A.M. Jeanneret, *Etrennes Neuchâteloises*, 1862.]

There are even verse narratives dedicated to the origins of horology. Works more mythological than historical ... or heroic histories. JeanRichard had five sons, all apprentices of their father, who went on to become master horologists. The peasant watchmaker and his large family took shape, becoming an authentic example of the ideal society. The watchmaker is a free man:

Secret power of a man of genius
A modern-day Vulcan, the apprentice JeanRichard
Will transform the fate of the mountain dweller...
[Louis Favre, 1869]

Double stoop at Crêt-Vaillant, Le Locle.

One can find popular patriotic novels in which there is a mixture of historical truth, myth and morality.

Here I am at the very source of this myth-history: how could anyone doubt, after reading such books, that the watchmaker is «born a watchmaker», that he embraces his career essentially out of a sense of «vocation», that he is blessed with «genius» and that, a perfect autodidact, he is a discover of «secrets», that he dies at his workbench, a tool in his hand?

I read on and find more and more surprising anecdotes; sometimes the history of watches can be summed up in telling comparisons. For example, it took Daniel JeanRichard nearly six months to make his first watch, but by 1837 it was possible to make a watch in just one day.

I understand that Neuchâtel watchmakers adapted themselves to the «vulgarisation» of their products, to an accessibility to the public stemming from the new working methods they employed (methods based on the principle of the division of labour, rationalisation, and mechanisation). The popularisation of time-pieces in the second half of the 19th century is associated with one name and a title, both very German-sounding – Georges-Louis Roskopf, the father of the «working man's watch». The Neuchâtel watchmaking industry continued to pursue its conquest of the world.

Since you're interested in the history of watchmaking in Le Locle, I'm sure that this little volume entitled «The Land of Micro-Precision» will fascinate you!

I am jolted from my reverie by Mr. Tissot, the head of the library. *It's the booklet published on the occasion of the centenary of the Charles Tissot & Sons SA factory in Le Locle in 1953!*

Daniel JeanRichard and the horse trader.
The Land of Micro-Precision, Tissot, 1953

Well! Well! If the authors of the 19th century tried, through history, to perpetuate the patrician values traditionally associated with watchmaking in order to moralise and to edify their contemporaries, I have to admit that they succeeded and that their fervent speeches are echoed even in the present day!

The Jura in the snow.
The Land of Micro-Precision, Tissot, 1953.

You'll see that the pride of the people here, the librarian continues, *perpetuates unchanging values linked to the exercise of their profession. People now talk about «horological culture» and contemporary historians are busy analysing its characteristics. But, just between me and you, you have to wonder what kind of thing is going to come out of their new approach.*

The brochure, covered in grey cloth, embellished with colour wash designs, illustrates once more the legend of Daniel JeanRichard and provides portraits of his descendants active in the professional establishments of the mid-20th century. It confirms the importance of horology for the town of Le Locle. Even in the cold, snowy winter one could enjoy the warmth of the workshop and the serene tranquillity and affable welcome of the watchmaker.

It's winter, it's biting cold, but what a comforting surprise … the sky is blue, the sun shines splendidly and you hardly think about the poor people you left down there in the mist! On the crest of the mountain, near a pine grove, is to be found one of the most modern and attractive factories to be seen in Switzerland: CHs. Tissot & Fils SA. Let's go in!
[Bolliger Hans, *The Centenary of the Charles Tissot & Fils SA Watch Factory. In the Land of Micro-Precision*, Zurich, 1953.]

The factory visit begins with a taste of the family atmosphere pervading the craft. *A little history…* concludes with a portrait of the members of the founding family – only the men, in fact, looking seriously into the camera's lens – all of whom had passed away by the time the book was published.

People throughout the region consider it a privilege to work at Tissot. Sometimes, when the grandfather retires, it's the father, or even the grandson or granddaughter, who takes his place. That creates a kind of positive atmosphere that is very easy to recognise, a kind of family spirit. That's how, in spite of mechanisation, the healthy tradition of the trade perpetuates itself.

The trade has been perfecting itself for two hundred and fifty years, helped along by the most intelligent of people and by an ever-alert creative spirit.

It is time to put the books and the brochure away. I go back to the hotel – *Les Trois Rois* – to which my guiding star has gently led me.

However, the image of an advertisement in black and white, covering an entire page now yellowed by the years, comes back to me: *Tissot, Switzerland's favourite watch.*

Read in books, taught and learned at school, events are chosen, classified, put in order – history begins the moment that social memory, the memory of men and women, fades away.

I fine-tune the preliminaries of my inquiry: what will the former Tissot employees teach me, what will the company's present directors tell me of the future? Who knows what I might have to say about my visit to the vast factory situated in the south of Le Locle's industrial zone?

There exist a number of documents from which I can learn the details of the factory's history. I do not know where they are to be found; I am not even certain how many there are, whether they abound in useful information, or are discreet to the point of silence.

I hope to be able to consult them without restriction. And I hope that I do not misrepresent them.

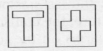

This morning, after having been here a few hours, I can immediately confirm certain data. The present-day town of Le Locle is a witness, at least visually, to the accelerated development of the watch industry here in the second quarter of the 19th century. In several neighbourhoods, the houses, with their rows of gables providing light for the watchmakers' workshops, are arranged in geometrical patterns on the slopes and folds of the valley that spreads out towards the French border.

My reading of these elements of architecture and town planning is easily reconcilable with the synthesis I have concocted from my more literary researches.

Would you like to peruse what I have scrupulously noted here, in the manner of a diligent student?

From 1740 onwards, the work done at home by the Neuchâtel watchmaker started to loosen its ties with the tasks associated with the world of agriculture; the craftsmen spread out across the vast farms on the foothills around Le Locle and began to find employment in the workshops springing up in the town itself. The land increasingly became a source of financial yield or supplementary earnings.

The watchmaking industry experienced an intense period of growth, characterised by an ever more sophisticated division of labour and by sustained expansion which continued until the French Revolution.

This phase corresponded to what was known as the «broken parts» system, similar to the *Verlagsystem* developed and practised in German-speaking Switzerland, where a trader with up-to-date knowledge of the market would supply primary materials to the workers through an *établisseur* who worked as a middleman and was responsible for co-ordinating the production process in a number of small centres.

The role of the *établisseur* was an important one; it was he who accurately forecast what would sell in particular markets, what was required by particular clients, and, indeed, which products would not be saleable at a given time.

The wages of the watchmakers were distributed twice a year, in autumn on St Martin's Day and in summer on St George's Day. This kind of work structure in the watchmaking industry, in which commerce held the upper hand over manufacture, lasted until the second half of the 19th century and gave birth to the modern workshop and the factory, separate from the home and increasingly mechanised.

Fountain in Le Locle, mid-19th century.

The expansion of the Neuchâtel watchmaking industry is revealed by the constant growth in the number of watchmakers in the villages of the mountains and the Val-de-Travers; amongst them were a certain number of workers from other Swiss regions, including many from Geneva, who were attracted by the absence of corporations and the liberal ways of the area. In the major watchmaking centres, such as Le Locle, La Chaux-de-Fonds and Fleurier, growth in the industry was a major factor in demographic expansion.

As a mnemonic aid, I have underlined two dates and two figures. In 1836, 160,000 watches made in Le Locle and La Chaux-de-Fonds were put on the market. In 1844, the corresponding figure was 280,000.

I have also found an amusing and forthright piece of advice: *'You big lug, if you want to die from hunger, then learn to be a cobbler, but if you want to become something, be a watchmaker. If you're nimble with the [lacemaker's] cushion, you'll earn money at the workbench. Just look at all the idiots who manage to earn spadefuls of gold.' It's true that the mid-19th century was a good time for the watchmaker's trade.*

[«Propos de Dentelle», in *Nouvelles Etrennes neuchâteloises*, Neuchâtel, 1914.]

It's the Town Chancellor, responsible for keeping the ancient archives of Le Locle, who cleverly sums up for me a story covering hundreds of years:

The local authorities, especially those set up after the founding of the Republic in 1848, provided a framework for the work and creative efforts of the

O. Huguenin, *The Watchmaker at his Workbench*,
circa 1850.

*town's watchmakers. They encouraged innovation
in production techniques and professional training.
All that led to the development of a stable industrial
structure in Neuchâtel. Judge for yourself:*

- *large watch firms see the light of day*
- *first workshops, then factories producing spare
  parts are set up (assortments, hairsprings, jewels,
  ébauches, cases, dials, etc.)*
- *training is organised around the new horological
  colleges opened in Le Locle (1868) and La
  Chaux-de-Fonds (1865) and around the
  Technicum (1933)*
- *infrastructure is developed, railways are built*
- *innovation and research are encouraged in the
  area by the Society of Patriotic Emulation (1791),
  the Neuchâtel Astronomical Observatory (1858)
  and the Laboratory of Horological Research,
  which opened in Neuchâtel in 1921*
- *these developments receive the financial support
  of the banks*
- *bosses and workers found their respective unions
  and confront one another, notably during the
  general strike of 1918, over working conditions.*

I never stop taking notes, scribbling hastily
away in my little book. Who knows? One day I
might publish a history of watchmaking in Le
Locle!

In fact, I am astounded by all this economic,
social, professional, cultural, even technical
and scientific ferment. I learn little-known

facts and am intrigued by their originality and density, which encourage me to study them further.

I note that in 1853, an impressive 142,717 gold watches and 164,678 silver ones were produced in the Neuchâtel Mountains and the Val-de-Travers, the valley below these peaks, which spreads out to the Franco-Swiss border at Les Verrières. It should be added that several hundred thousand watch movements were also produced.

Were I a graphic artist, a mathematician or an accountant, I would amuse myself by drawing exponential curves. This would provide a very gratifying exercise for Neuchâtel watchmakers, even if it would inevitably feature some substantial downturns caused by economic crises, the closing of borders, and obstacles to exports. An exercise in interpretation too, if I think of the dwindling profits, the epidemics, the periods of high unemployment – hard times which alternated with periods of prosperity and ease.

Thanks to a brief conversation with a 90-year-old gentleman seated at a table in the Café de la Place du Marché, I am better able to understand why the watchmakers persisted in their trade, why they never gave up, despite the hard knocks meted out to their industry by the recurrent crises.

The old man tells me: *Horology consists of 'savoir-faire'; for this very reason, it's a fragile industry. It's an exportable industry, and when it's exported it exposes itself to many risks. But, sir, it's the value of this same 'savoir-faire' that anchors the industry to our mountains. You'll be amazed to learn that horology is made up of more than a hundred different trades. ... Are you familiar with the expression 'broken parts'? It refers to the organisation of work into different trades. When I was an apprentice, I made escapements. I still keep my tools in the room upstairs, the tools that the master gave me when I finished my apprenticeship.*

Am I mistaken, or do I detect a note of pride in the old man's voice? *Of course, if the case makers were the 'Barons', the setters were the aristocrats of watchmakers! Excuse me, sir ... er, Prince,* I mumble, novice in the subject that I am.

Let us continue. Le Locle's 19th century development is characterised by a lively, lush climate of creativity, production and training. The confectioner in whose shop I have just tasted a delicious chocolate tells me that the famous Klaus caramels have been made in Le Locle since the mid-19th century. Thus Suchard and Klaus are both part of Neuchâtel's gastronomic – and industrial – heritage.

I am also able, thanks to information supplied by the Commune's architect, to tell you that, in 1893, the authorities decided to introduce a new street numbering system in Le Locle – with even numbers on the right and odd numbers on the left, starting from the top of the street in both cases.

Le Locle, circa 1920.
Astra Aero Aviation Suisse SA, Zurich.

My curiosity piqued, I read the enamel plaques on the buildings.

I have never concentrated my attention on such a wealth of symbols. The street names are eloquent: Progress Street, Industry Street, Concord Street, Peace Street …

The town walls, rebuilt after the fire of 1833, reveal Le Locle's political colours, its socialist tendencies, its workers' unions, its ambitious employers' associations.

After Rue JeanRichard, Rue Henry Grandjean and the Grande Rue, I start up the Crêt Vaillant, which is slightly further up the slope. The heavy-looking buildings are solidly set on their broad foundations. Fine stairways lead up to them, small gardens and fountains line their façades.

A feline shape slips agilely through a wooden cat-flap. Its shining eyes observe me curiously. *What on earth is this ridiculous tourist doing here, nosing around the place and stumbling over the paving stones!*

Ridiculous maybe, but not blind! A glinting object next to some wide, irregularly shaped blocks cut from Jura limestone attracts my gaze. It's an engraved bronze plaque on the façade of N° 23, *Formerly the residence of Charles-Félicien Tissot and of his son, Charles-Emile. The watch factory Chs Tissot & Fils was founded here in 1853.*

A tall man, mature and placid, quietly walks up to me. Without introducing himself, he begins to talk.

I'm the man who attached the plaque, sir. I ordered it a few years ago from a foundryman in Bienne. It was paid for by the Tissot management. I've got a little tale to tell about it.

We're leaning against the drystone wall surrounding the garden at Crêt-Vaillant N° 23. The rising sun diffuses a soft light.

Thus I learn, almost by chance, that I have happened upon the very first page of the history of Tissot watches, the very history that is the object of my excursion.

«On this site was founded, in 1853,
the watch factory, Chs Tissot & Son…»

Charles-Félicien Tissot, known as Daguette – that is his full name – was born in Le Locle in 1804; although a proud bourgeois citizen of Valangin, he is originally from Le Locle.

He practises the trade of gold case-maker, which means that he is something of a goldsmith and something of a mechanic, making the cases housing the movements of pocket watches. Since his marriage at the town's temple to Julie, his betrothed, the life of Charles-Félicien has become busier, and on 29th November 1828 he becomes the father of a daughter, Adèle. In 1830, the little family welcomes the arrival of Charles-Emile, and, three years later, of Auguste.

The Tissots' tall house on Crêt-Vaillant overlooks the Rue du Marais facing the rising sun which warms our bones today. In 1844, the building not only housed the family of the case-maker, but also the *guillochage* workshop (the term refers to the mechanical engraving of watch cases) belonging to Monsieur Grivaz.

And there is Charles-Emile, already on the point of finishing his schooling. He is 12 and has informed his father of his desire to become a watchmaker. He is looking for an apprenticeship in the village and in his juvenile enthusiasm he is already thinking of travelling abroad to improve his skills. He has found a fixed engraver's burin, a vice, and some tweezers. His mother smiles, sewing the hem of the grey smock customary for the apprentice watchmaker. His father needs no convincing, he knows that his son is taking up a trade

Crêt-Vaillant N° 23, Le Locle.

TISSOT DAGUETTE

Charles Félicien
1804-1873

Adèle
1828

Charles Emile
1830-1910

Auguste
1833

Paul
1835

Emma
1846

Charles
1860-1936

[Paul] Edouard
1864-1939

Paul
1890-1951

Marie
1897-1980

Edouard Louis
1896-1977

Renée

Hélène

Anna Gabriela
1929

Henriette Renée
1930

Luc Edouard
1937

Delphine Irène
1941

which will guarantee him a good living, as long as he is dextrous, has good eyes and is gifted with sharp hearing.

Charles-Emile's father is ambitious. Perhaps he has the intuition that this would be a propitious time to open a branch and have his son work there.

Charles-Félicien puts on his new formal suit and ties his black tie. He goes to the notary's office in the spring of 1846 to sign the purchase contract on a *parcel of land* to add to his property at Vaillant Crest.

In 1848, shortly after the revolution that installed a republican government in the Château of Neuchâtel, Charles-Emile went to New York to work for his uncle Charles-Emile Humbert Droz as a repairer. The inventory of tools that he took with him still exists; the tall man explains it to me, reciting the contents:

The total amounts to 3,454.3 batz, plus a watch to the value of 334 batz and a large trunk with a lock to the value of 58 batz (the old Neuchâtel currency).

But follow me. I want to show you the Tissot family archives. They're in a loft and I am responsible for keeping the keys. But we need to go up to the site of the factory in the Rue des Tourelles. Look, it's just opposite us, right over there!

In my notebook, I've sketched a charming little scene: blue and grey cardboard boxes, black ledgers on a pine counter, an elegant brass oil lamp with a link shade, a heavy platform scale and, in the background, placed in a long line beneath the windows, a series of workbenches over which the backs of three watchmakers are bent.

The Tissot «Comptoir», circa 1890.

A «timing-cupboard» is attached to a wall covered in wooden slats. It is the place where the newly regulated watches are kept under observation [before final dispatch].

A birdcage hangs from a beam which follows the slope of the roof; the song of the canary inside accompanies the long sessions of the finishers. We move on to the realms of the case-maker, the watchmaker and the *établisseur*.

Orders are managed by the person in charge of *établissage*, but Charles-Félicien leaves to his wife, an efficient colleague, the responsibility for writing entries in the purchase and sales ledgers. The accounting system is a simple one; all that needs to be done is to balance the books in just the same way as the schoolteacher shows the local pupils, who practise the method in class. The nib of the quill pen scratches across the lined paper. Behind the counter, there is a row of round jars with labels of all sizes tied to them, indicating the cardboard boxes to be delivered, the crates to be shipped.

Crates for Russia must not be over 4½ feet long
1 foot 2 inches wide
1 foot high and weigh 82 Swiss ounces.

Crates for South America must be secured with straps and require two declarations and a waybill.

For direct deliveries to Russia,
the following items are required:
2 [customs] declarations in German
2 in French
and a waybill.

For Germany, a waybill is required, as are:
2 declarations in French
1 in German
Letters for Buenos Aires must weigh 7½ grams.

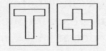

We have travelled from the shop to the factory, and here we are on the south-facing slope of the valley. *How natural it feels to navigate through Time like this, without being overly concerned about the rules of chronology,* I think to myself. *But we should not let ourselves get lost!*

The Tissot factory, Le Locle, 1907-1962.

The voluble guardian of the keys to the Tissot loft hands me a copy of the *Feuille d'Avis des Montagnes* a newspaper published in Neuchâtel in July 1853, for me to read the following lines. It doesn't take me long to spot the similarities with a certain page in a magazine I leafed through on the train.

What about you, do you remember it?

Art Deco Tissot watches,
Revue Internationale de l'Horlogerie, 1923.

The citizens Charles-Félicien Tissot, case-maker, and his son Charles-Emile Tissot, watchmaker, have together formed an association under the trading name Charles-Félicien Tissot & Fils.

This association, the aim of which is to do business in the watchmaking trade, was formed on 1ˢᵗ July of this year and has been authorised for a period of five years up to 1ˢᵗ July 1858.

The craftsmen who work at home (escapement makers, *faiseurs de secrets*, finishers, enamellers and so on) are attracted to the Crêt-Vaillant address by the jobs offered by the Tissots; they complete these same jobs a few weeks later and deliver the finished product in blue cardboard boxes each containing a dozen pieces.

Frédéric Ulysse grew old late in life, finishing escapements by the flickering light of his oil lamp.

«Listen, lad! Take these big boxes to Old Man Tissot ... and be quick about it! This cream cake fresh out of the oven will be waiting for you...»

With meticulous care, the dextrous watchmakers make the fine pieces Charles-Emile then tries to sell during a 43 year career including 52 long journeys which take him to the Americas and to Russia. During his interminable absences, which amount to a total of seven years of peregrinations, his wife runs the shop in Le Locle and brings up their sons Charles and Paul Edouard, born in 1860 and 1864 respectively.

In my notebook, I have entered Charles-Emile Tissot's first journey to North America under the year 1848. The event is documented by a passage in a passport registered in Neuchâtel: *Monsieur Charles-Emile Tissot, watchmaker in Le Locle, domiciled there, a citizen of this republic, going to France and elsewhere, height five feet one inch, aged 18 years and 6 months, light brown hair and eyebrows, average nose, average mouth, light growth of beard, round chin, oval face, pale complexion.*

Pale complexion! But isn't it said that travel broadens the mind of youth?

Old Man Henchoz often told us the story. When Paul Tissot came back from New York in 1921, after his first prospecting trip to America, he had with him a pile of orders and ten large cases full of cigarettes and tins of pineapple … The employees, the work-men and the suppliers each bought a few of these exotic goods. A stock of cigars proved harder to place.

Here. How much do you think this lovely 18 carat gold repeater weighs? I'll tell you – it weighs 132.5 grams. It was made in 1883 for the Klumak Brothers of Vienna, «Brüder Klumak, Wien, Chronometer-macher der KK Kriegs Marine», agents of the Tissot company in the Austro-Hungarian Empire.

As soon as I have the watch, with its cover open, in the palm of my hand, it starts to chime in ringing tones: one, two, three, four, five … a hammer taps lightly on the gong to mark the passing hours.

I shiver a little.

My guide is making himself busy. He grabs a few boxes and opens them up to show me some examples of the pocket watches sent around the world by the Tissot company from 1853 on. He says: *It is estimated that in the eleven months following its creation, the company delivered around 1,150 finished pieces to Le Locle. Look, you can see them mentioned there in the first large éta-blissage. Today, I estimate that we've sold over 35 million watches! I'm very proud.*

Look, the dials have different brands on them.

That's because when Charles-Félicien Tissot died in 1873, the company name was changed to «Charles Tissot Favre Locle»,to celebrate, as is the custom, the marriage between Charles-Emile and Françoise Sophie Amélie née Favre.

Tissot pocket watches,
Revue Internationale de l'Horlogerie, 1923.

Opening more cases, I discover other names: *Charles-Emile Tissot Locle* and *Charles-Emile Tissot & Fils, Le Locle, Charles Tissot & Fils* and even *«Tissot Watches Le Locle-Genève».*

A little dazed by all these mysterious objects which offer themselves to the touch of my clumsy fingers, I turn to reach for a slim volume bound in real leather, its spine marbled with coloured grains: *What a lovely book!*

Tissot 116 Calibre, circa 1928.

It's the *Supplier Day Book*, the register of all the craftsmen from whom the Tissots ordered *ébauches*, finished movements, or specific finishing jobs. By the dim glow diffused by the skylight, I decipher the finely written entries embellished with elegant initial letters: *Japy Brothers of Beaucourt, Bueche Boillat of Reconvillier, Aubert Brothers and Audemars Frères, E. Francillon.*

The register's columns are filled with picturesque names. I content myself with reading them off without attempting to grasp their exact meanings – fusee chronometers, stopwatches with independent second hands, split-seconds chronographs, complicated and lunar phase watches, key wound movements, aperture watches...

I turn the heavy pages.

- Look! Between 1860 and 1875, the Tissot company not only produced finished watches, but also all kinds of spare parts, watchmaking tools, keys, hydraulic watch hammers and oils, razors, watch chains, fine brooches, lockets, tie-pins....

- But, tell me, does anyone know what all these pieces finished by the company look like?

- Alas, only a few ancient production ledgers are left to give us an idea of the cases decorated with enamel motifs (cannons, eagles, guns...). The influence of Art Nouveau and Art Deco is noticeable at the turn of the century... I see that you're not entirely convinced.

A number of magnificent catalogues printed in the 1920s are laid out before me: the Tissot cases are decorated with engravings of flowers in pink niello. I can pick out stylised cyclamens, roses, marguerites, floral garlands, shields edged with flowers. There are yet other designs engraved in gold, there are patterned jewels and rose-cut diamonds on polished metal, grey-blue enamelled rosettes and «electric grey» enamelled festoons.

- Who had the idea of photographing some of these charming little pendant watches for ladies?

Enamelled Tissot watches, circa 1900.

- There, sir, you touch upon one of the most fascinating pages of the history of Tissot; I refer, sir, to the prosperous Russian period, brutally curtailed by the first revolution of February-March 1917, and definitively ended by the Bolshevik Revolution of October 1917.

The tone is grave. The twilight hour creates an atmosphere that encourages the sharing of confidences.

The archivist dedicated to Tissot first shows me a small black and white photograph.

It is Miss Marie Tissot who cuts the cake offered to her to celebrate her 50 years of activity within the company.

Marie Tissot celebrating
with Mr. Weibel and Mr. Schatz, 1966.

He then tells me of Charles's establishment in Moscow in the late 1880s, of his marriage to Marie Fadieff, of the birth of Paul in 1890 and Marie in 1897. Marie's name can be found in the parish register of the Church of the Annunciation in Petrovsky Park.

Date of Birth: 25ᵗʰ June/7ᵗᵗʰ July; Date Baptised: 6ᵗʰ July [1897]

Marie, daughter of Swiss Citizen Charles Tissot Daguette, of the Reformed Evangelical confession, and his legitimate wife, Marie Vassiligeva, an Orthodox Russian.

Godparents: the Moscow bourgeois of the district, Alex. [Alexander] Nicolas Timofeyev Mestcheriakov and the widow of the son of the Moscow merchant, Anna Timofeyeva Gorojankin. The priest performing the baptism: Priest of the Parish Piotr Speranzky with the church clergy. I hereby certify the authenticity of the signature of Mr. N. Triaguin, notary of the Moscow Stock Exchange, 9/31 October 1898.

Then he shows me the yellowed photograph of the Tchetunov brothers' shop in Illinka Street where Tissot watches were offered to the whims and caprices of Moscow's middle classes.

Outside the Tissot shop at 5, Illinka Street, Moscow.

He continues: *On various occasions, Charles-Emile travelled from Koenigsberg to St. Petersburg by dog sleigh, a journey that lasted three days and two nights. His register contains the details of the watch collections he was going to sell at the Nizhni Novgorod fair.*

His grandchildren recounted his adventures for many years afterwards; the fear of wolves, travelling by simple tarantass, the arrogance displayed by the clients to the young Swiss supplier ... payments made in gold ingots and cases of tea. But his son Charles continued the courageous efforts of his father up until 1901.

Carefully, my informant takes a heavy pocket-watch from its case. It is similar to the ones that the Le Locle company produced at the beginning of the 20th century for the officers of the various Russian Imperial regiments, embellished with inscriptions, allegories and coats-of-arms.

The watch of the Tsar, he announces solemnly.

He takes some bundles of Russian roubles and German marks from a dusty cardboard box; in a slim waxed canvas wallet there is an unused reserve of Russian postage stamps. Nicholas II's rigid bearing is absolutely appropriate to his status as Emperor!

Envelope and models for engravings
destined for the Russian market, circa 1900.

From another box, my guide takes a large, slightly rounded wristwatch and says with a smile, *It's a banana watch!* At least he's certain to attract my attention.

It's a historic piece. It came back to Le Locle to be repaired, but after the events of 1917 it was illegal to send it back. In 1991, it was restored and now features in the catalogue as a faithful reproduction called «Classic Prince». It is very popular with our modern-day Russian customers … especially with the young men. It has style, don't you think?

Objects from history …

Did I tell you about my grandfather's watch?

A memory, other memories ….

Another anecdote, sir, about Marie, the lady whose English teapot can be seen on a shelf in the loft, with a pin-cushion and a revolving case for displaying photographs.

This is Mademoiselle Marie …
Walking through the workshops and offices with dainty steps, she hugs the yellow wage packets under her arm. Her accountant, is obliged to be present every Saturday, be it rainy or overcast, that Marie Tissot is unable to go to La Claire Roche and her cabin at the Alpine Club. *We have work to do*, the woman sometimes known as «The Empress» says into the telephone. Strict, serious and obstinate, she nevertheless has a smile on her face when she sees her employees in the basement or at the back of the offices boiling a kettle or making up their dresses for the Christmas party of 1950. People know that while others enjoy the festivities, she herself, busy and attentive, will be at home in the Rue de Tourelles making clothes for some new-born baby.

It is time to close the loft's doors.

We will return here tomorrow.
Good night, sir, and thank you for your kindness.

Early that morning I climb the long narrow flight of steps leading up to the factory.

Out of breath and attempting to avoid the innumerable snails strewn over the dew-covered stones, I stop at the foot of a modern building before beginning my tour of the domain. And what a vast domain it is! It includes several distinct wings, constructed at different periods. Listing them from east to west: 1907, 1917, 1929, 1947, 1961, 1965…

I am careful not to omit 2002; the façades are being renovated and the scaffolding surrounding the South Tower covers them with a green mask.

For Tissot's real estate faithfully mirrors the company's evolution: from the original firm with its ten employees, to the modern enterprise which, by the end of the 1960s, provided work for over 1,000 people.

I have in my hand the brochure in which this information is laid out. The little book also includes the instructions given to the *concierge* of the first factory in 1911.

Tissot advertisement, *Indicateur Davoine,*
La Chaux-de-Fonds, 1913.

1. Sweep the workshops, the stairs, and all the rooms in the factory every day; make sure to push the chests of drawers back and brush under them.

2. Wax the workbenches every Saturday.

3. Make sure that the desks are particularly clean.

4. Wax and repair the linoleum in the offices and

workshops every month. Mats and carpets must be beaten on the bar specifically installed for the purpose and not on the lawn. (…)

5. Empty and wash the spittoons twice a week.

6. Clean the factory windows twice a year. A woman will be hired to help the concierge *with this task.(…)*

When the workmen leave at midday, the concier-

The Tissot buildings in 1929.

ge *will open the factory windows and close them again at 1 o'clock.*

I turn the pages.

In 1977, the company was based in three different geographical locations and employed 690 people: La Chaux-de-Fonds [Factory III, assembly] and Peseux [Industrial Production Centre] are the watch production centres.

In Le Locle are gathered together under a single roof watch production, ébauches, synthetic materials [Factory II], the sales company covering Switzerland, the production back-up team and the administrative department.

A loud voice startles me from my reverie.

The Tissot domain in 1961.

- Don't forget to go back over your notes and include the Foyer Tissot in your report! Remember, it was inaugurated on 20th April 1949. The establishment provided full board or single meals to the factory employees at very modest prices. I should point out, however, that the managers and the workers did not eat at the same table... Guess who the napkins and the arrangements of wild flowers were for!

- Good morning! You're an early riser!

110

- It's a habit with watchmakers – at the workbench by 7 a.m.! But in fact, I'm no more than a kind of functionary, a salesman, that's all!

My guide of the previous day is keen to pursue our exploration of the domain. Without pausing, he goes on:

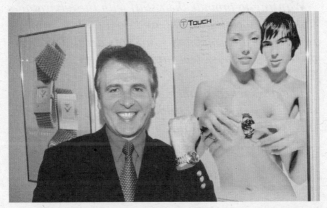

François Thiébaud, President of Tissot, 2001.

After our visit to the loft, I'll introduce you to our director.
Let me refresh your memory?
The Le Locle factory, which has been actively renovated and refurbished, is home to three brands owned by the Swatch Group: Tissot, Certina and Mido have been directed by the same team since 1996 with Mr. François Thiébaud, as their President.

The clocking-on machine in the factory entrance seems to me to be extremely simple compared to the heavy machines of the last century with their perforated cards – machines that look like the outsized roulette wheels one sees at fun fairs.

Wanting to provide their staff with the advantages linked to social progress and to improve working conditions, the company's directors decided to introduce a flexitime system throughout the enterprise in 1971.

The days when workers marched from the town to the factory in serried ranks are long gone... Look, this is the tiny little office of the lady who checked the staff when they came in and went out.

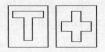

On the sixth floor of the North Tower, the President is busy reading the introduction to a book which is being printed. It's a new history of Tissot, part of the series of events marking the 150th anniversary of the founding of the factory – events the President himself and his executive committee have organised to celebrate the year 2003.

You haven't forgotten, I imagine? 1853–2003.

Mr. Thiébaud welcomes me eagerly, inquiring about the reason for my visit. He begins to give me a methodical introduction to «his factory».

The Tissot archives are spread out over various collections kept in a number of different locations. We are working on concentrating them all in one place, on inventorying them and finding an adequate site in which they can be conserved and consulted.

113

You should bear in mind that the archives are hard to access, because, in 1925, Tissot signed a commercial partnership agreement with the two brothers Louis and Gustave Brandt, directors of the Omega company in Bienne. This original partnership led to the setting up of a holding company, la Société Suisse pour l'Industrie Horlogère *(Swiss Society for the Horology Industry, SSIH, 1930), which later formed an association and then merged with ASUAG in 1983. In 1985 it became a part of* la Société Suisse de Microélectronique et d'horlogerie *(Swiss Microelectronics Company, SMH, 1985), which itself took the new company name of The Swatch Group in 1998.*

- In fact, Mr. Thiébaud, my research has already led me to discover that the history of Tissot is marked by a large number of different company names.

I proudly exhibit my notebook, which contains the exact chronology.

From Charles-Félicien Tissot to Charles-Emile Tissot & Fils (1865) and Chs. Tissot & Fils SA (1917), SSIH (1930), Tissot Marché Suisse SA (1976 – which was reintegrated into Tissot SA in 1982), and Tissot Synthétic (1979–1985).

In the SSIH–ASUAG merger of 1983, the setting up of the *Société Suisse de Microélectronique et d'Horlogerie* (SMH) in 1985 and the introduction of the name Swatch Group in 1998, one figure stands out – Nicolas G. Hayek, an important personage in the present-day set-up of Tissot SA.

It's true. We owe a good deal to the confidence and support of Nicolas Hayek. Without him, who knows what would have become of an old brand like Tissot, which was badly shaken by the consequences of the crisis of 1975 and of the many restructurings that it has undergone.

Tissot *ébauche* workers, circa 1940.

François Thiébaud walks towards the luminous bay windows of his office, from where he is able to enjoy a breathtaking view of Le Locle. His tone is enthusiastic.

I want to make the people who work for Tissot happy. I also want to motivate the people who love this company, stimulate creativity and the collective spirit, encourage employees to identify with their firm. We must get those active in the local horological cultural heritage involved, because that heritage is undeniably exceptional.

The telephone rings, interrupting the President briefly.

I quickly realise that the desire to mark the 150th anniversary of the creation of the Tissot watch company Le Locle coincides with a project to protect the local industrial heritage. Through his attachment to the project and his encouraging recognition of past efforts, through his well-developed respect for the values of hard work, François Thiébaud, who has been devoted – he points out – to the Tissot cause since 1996, reveals his admiration for a company that was, in the 1970s, the region's largest employer.

He wants to share his pride in belonging to a long-term project based on the efforts of thousands of people and he also wants to demonstrate his ambitions for the future, which he hopes will be as glorious as the past.

Tissot thus possesses a historical fortune – and a history most of whose chapters are yet to be written – unmatched by most of its competitors. My curiosity is awakened.

The telephone rings again.

And shortly thereafter: *I'm taking you on a tour of the company. Would you like that?*

The telephone rings yet again.

Mr. Thiébaud then presents me with another guide, a pretty, elegant lady, small and smiling. She is the Human Resources Director.

I take leave of my host, thanking him for his kindness. He presents me with a Swiss Army knife. Thank you! He also gives me two very small, abundantly illustrated original catalogues full of information about Tissot past and present. A very good idea.

And then a number of representatives of the management welcome a class of schoolchildren who have made the journey from Ascona, a little town in the heart of the Ticino, to discover the region and its living industrial heritage – the Tissot factory is an ideal observation point, welcoming and generous.

There's a commotion on the stairs. The kids are excited about the free baseball caps they have received displaying the Tissot logo. They pose proudly for the photographer sent by the local paper *L'Impartial* to immortalise their visit. The cheerful young English PR executive finds their enthusiasm infectious. She is delighted, *It's great!...*

We open our doors to visitors … it's a tradition of ours, my new guide tells me. *There was even a slogan about it in the 1970s:* «Come in and look around, it's the best way of convincing you of the quality of our watches». *At that time our Open Days were aimed at the families and friends of Tissot employees: 3,500 people came in October 1970. I'll show you the photos of the children letting the balloons off!*

We pass rows of workbenches at which serious-minded trainees are working. The sight of them reminds me of the delicate aquatints of an 18th century apprentice watchmaker from German-speaking Switzerland painted while he was in Le Locle, pictures of the backs of studious apprentices by the window, seated in rows beside their master.

My guess is confirmed by my guide, who tells me: *This is our training centre, where watch retailers come from all over the world for personalised courses on Tissot products. Really, it's not easy to grasp all the subtleties of the advanced technology of the T-Touch. It's even harder to explain them to a potential customer. We help our students to conquer these difficulties.*

We stride purposefully through the Reception & Dispatch Department, the advertising material warehouse, the offices of the Accounts Department, the Decoration

Department and the offices responsible for the «Swiss market».

I take a particular interest in the Products Department; I dream of casting an eye over a prototype, an embryonic watch. What a joy to be so close to a secret…

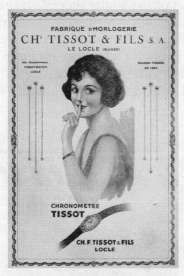

Tissot advertisement, 1923.

My guide has read my mind and mischievously recites a clause from an old contract: *Visitors will undertake not to reveal the production processes used in the company and to observe the strictest discretion concerning all technical and commercial aspects…*

I am surprised that Research & Development Department is not full of drafting tables: *Since the introduction of computers, they have become nothing but a distant memory.*

Here we are at the «Department of Pocket Watches and Advanced Component-Making».

The sight of the many pieces on their trays is all the confirmation I need of the dynamism of this department. By chance, I find a catalogue: the 1999 replica collection includes some 50 models in a wide range of styles (chrome, silver-plated and gold-plated metal, silver and gold).

Heritage Collection, 1999.

But what are all these 'replicas'? It all sounds a bit reminiscent of Blade Runner *to me.*

A blonde lady raises her head and smiles at my perplexity. She replies graciously: *You're funny! Allow me to explain. The word «Replica» was chosen to describe pocket watches with modern, often quartz, movements, based on «historic»pieces.*

Heritage Collection, 2001.

She takes a drawing of a lady's round pocket watch, a little «bonbon» gliding along a satin bracelet, and continues: *Certain wristwatches, based on old models, have been assigned to the «Testimonial» and «Heritage» collections. In that way we can present successful models such as the PR516 of the mid-1960s, the marvellous chronographs of the 1940s, and the pieces designed during the Belle Époque.*

She hands me an attractive barrel watch, the Porto, similar to a piece I saw yesterday in the collection of old timepieces, more a pocket watch, a «skeleton movement» whose finely made gearing can be seen through the glass.

It should be underlined that, since its creation, Tissot has always produced pocket watches. Even now it is the world's leading producer of that particular item, a privileged witness to the long history of the Swiss watch industry.

We continue our visit.

I catch someone talking quietly about the victory of a certain football team – it's the middle of the World Cup and the Summer Solstice!

Did you know that England's talented goal-scorer Michael Owen is an ambassador for Tissot?

Paul Tissot in the factory workshops, circa 1948.

In fact, I have seen his face in the displays in retailers' shop windows. Am I going to let myself be tempted into buying a limited edition watch featuring the name of Europe's 2001 Footballer of the Year?

We have crossed the footbridge linking the factory's two main buildings.

We enter the workshop area.

Good morning, ladies and gentlemen!

Indistinct voices murmur their replies. We are not sure whether we should disturb the calm of this special place. It seems that I should, from now on, speak to my guide in a whisper.

But, you know, in the past, the workshops were full of clear and joyous song, she tells me. Humming a popular melody, she begins to recount a brief anecdote.

«Gentle ferrywoman, leave your boat there...»

In the workshop, circa 1960.

Paul Tissot parks the comfortable car in which he has travelled to Bienne. He has just visited his watch factory. In so doing, he is able to forget his role as Sales Director of Omega Watches for a while and come back to «La Tissot», the firm founded by his forebears and run, during the week, by his capable sister, «Little Marie».

His black hat placed firmly on his head, Paul walks into the setters' workshop. Noticing the «boss» entrance, they fall silent: «Ladies, please ... don't stop singing, it's such a joy to listen to you».

It is 1936 and autumn is approaching. Unemployment is nearing its peak – 93,000 people in Switzerland are without work.

We are silent for a moment.

You know, a few years ago, when the head of personnel walked into a workshop, people became nervous and turned their eyes away ... as if the boss's appearance was synonymous with bad news, a reprimand, a warning or, even worse, a sacking ... It took some time for people to realise that I could just be enquiring about their health, about how they liked the job, about a child I'd heard was ill ... Didn't Marie Tissot and Jean Simon do the same!?

But she remembers her conversation with the now-retired workers from Tissot, Aciera, Zenith, Dixi, Fabriques d'Assortiments réunies and other companies.

They spoke bitterly of the years of crisis and unemployment – 1929, 1939, 1975, 1996. They also talked about the disarray of the directors, who, in spite of the economic constraints which seemed to have made all human emotion irrelevant, *felt unable to sack people!*

In our region, I said, *where metallurgy is very important, we have experienced the same kinds of problems. Unemployment, «rationalisation» of the workforce, closures ... broken equipment, abandoned factories.*

After the period of full employment, the years during which there was a shortage of local labour and skilful Italian and Spanish immigrants were welcomed to our mountains, we were cruelly hit. Do you realise that the company which employed 1,200 people shed half its workforce in just a few months? We now have some 600 people working here in Le Locle, out of a total of around 500 Tissot employees. Indeed, Tissot is implicated in thousands of other jobs around the world. Don't forget all the work required for production and assembly and finishing that is carried out by associated partners of the Swatch Group.

I stop to examine an unusual document, hanging from a nail in the wall, listing company regulations. The rules were co-signed in 1906 by «the boss», Charles-Emile Tissot, and two representatives of the workforce.

Art. 3   The normal working day is 10 hours long. This period is reduced to 9 hours on Friday and the day before holidays. The working day must finish by 5 p.m.

Art. 4   Any time not spent at work, for whatever reason, will be deducted from wages.

Art. 5   It is forbidden to enter or remain in the factory before or after working hours without express permission.

Art. 6   Male or female workers who are unable to

come to work or only able to come to work late or who leave work early must inform the director or the person standing in for him.

Art. 7 Repeated non-respect of working hours or infractions of the regulations, any lack of respect for the boss or lack of politeness between workers, any negligence in the care of one's tools, the introduction of fermented drinks on to the premises, rude conversation or songs, and all unauthorised movements between workshops are forbidden and can, if repeated, lead to the immediate dismissal of the worker in question without pay.

Art. 8 Wages will be distributed once a week on Saturdays.

Art. 9 These regulations, approved by the Council of State, will be printed and displayed in the workshops. All workers will receive a copy when they are hired.

My guide points out: *All this is relatively far from the content of the contracts of today's employees in the Swatch Group, at least literally, if not in spirit!*

Let's take a look at some of the clauses from the interwar period:

Art. 1.   The working day is 8¾ hours long, 4¼ hours on Saturdays and on the days before holidays. In summer it is 8¼ hours long, in winter 7¾ hours. The division of working hours is governed by a special schedule.

Art. 2.   Wages will be distributed every two weeks on Thursdays.

Art. 5.   It is the duty of all workers to dedicate their entire attention to the execution of the task entrusted to them; to take care of materials, machines, tools, and all the factory's equipment, to maintain cleanliness and to have respectful relationships with superiors and subordinates, as well as with the other workers in the establishment. Workers are responsible for all objects entrusted to them.

Art. 6.   All factory staff must make scrupulous use of the means designed to protect the health and lives of the workers and strictly observe all regulations established to this effect. It is forbidden to smoke in the factory, to spit on the floor, and to introduce alcoholic drinks on to the premises. Clothes and other objects must be kept in the facilities specifically provided for that purpose.

My guide further explains: *Our social policy is still based on the principles of vigilance and solidarity. We provide financial aid and material and moral support whenever necessary. We put a lot of effort into organising our summer soirées and Christmas parties. Also, active executives are at the service of retired workers, especially during the Open Days organised especially for them.*

I enjoy a delicious snack with Mr. Pius Felber at the cafeteria. He has contributed to the new decorations and tells me that he thinks it very important that the company premises should have a pleasant, fresh, dynamic atmosphere. He recently had a series of paintings hung, thus transforming the factory's corridors into an art gallery for a few days.

He keeps a close eye on the refurbishment of the buildings making up the Tissot domain. He is also taking an interest in the development of adequate conservation facilities for the company's archives.

The mention of a garage leads Pius Felber to a subject about which he is passionate – cars.

Pius Felber, Tissot Vice-President, 2002.

He tells me that there is a chauffeur's hat and uniform in the loft.

They belonged to Tissot's chauffeur, Charles – or Calli – Thomas, who took clients from the station to the Rue des Tourelles in the company's lovely black Ford. The veterans even remember having seen him ferry around the company's football team.

He continues: *My landlady is the daughter of a former Tissot Sales Director. She remembers the visits of the sales agents to Le Locle. Mr. Dorot from Paris, Mr. De Marchi from Turin, the Holzer brothers from New York and Mexico, the Sibner-Hegners, agents for Holland and Asia respectively … all of them had a lot of respect for Georges-Louis Weibel and were appreciative of the conviviality of his wife Marie and the welcome accorded them by the couple's young daughter, who waited for them in the Tissot Ford driven by the multi-talented Calli.*

We have both agreed to visit Madame the widow and Madame the daughter of the former Sales Director.

And I still have to talk to you about our motor racing sponsorship!

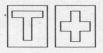

Driving down the Argillat road, I think about the working conditions in Le Locle in the early 20th century. I should mention that I have spent the evening reading a fascinating novel by a militant worker about the effects of the 1929 Wall Street Crash on the communities of the Jura Mountains: *A Smock Around Your Neck*.

The crisis is upon us and the workshops are emptying. Deserted premises echo with the strange and painful sound of solitude. Stools turned upside down seem to gesture imploringly. The machinery sleeps; greasy, tenacious dust settles on the gears, pulleys, and belts, taking advantage of their immobility while rust slyly eats away at the polished steel.

… And on the dismal wall of the cloakroom, surrounded by its companions, and like them abandoned, the neglected smock sleeps miserably.

I have learned that the authorities of Le Locle often sported socialist colours, that militant workers wore the characteristic wide-brimmed black hat. They confronted the liberal «Bedouins» and the very conservative local bourgeoisie.

But, even if the workers supported the local committee of the 1918 General Strike, I notice that they preferred to take part in the Workers' Theatre, where they put on *Topaze* and light comedies of a slightly saucy nature.

It's the era of worker education, the period when the Left wanted its own music societies, theatre troupes, gymnastics clubs, choirs and outings to the countryside: a vast cultural project accompanied by great expectations that were often disappointed. During the 1921–1922 recession, the same workers cut timber in the forest, happy to avoid having to sign on at the labour exchange.

It seems undeniable that the bosses at Tissot were characterised by their rigour and sobriety. Charles-Emile, especially, combined his professional responsibilities with a busy public life. His successors and their close collaborators contribute to Le Locle's political scene. Local politicians defend the interests of the region's watchmaking industry.

I'm hungry.

I stop off at the «Au Moka» café to try the fillet of perch advertised on the menu.

The restaurant is full and the establishment hums with happy conversation. The waiter leads me to the «singles tables».

Hello, ladies and gentlemen, I say as I take my place on the narrow bench.

You're not from the area, are you? But the fillet's worth the trip, you'll see. We have it every Friday. The owner knows what he's doing!

The well-presented dish contains an assortment of fillets of fish prepared *à la meunière:* a very popular meal in the Neuchâtel region, there's no doubt about it!

Monsieur Charles kicks off the conversation. *Can I pour you some coffee?*

Monsieur Charles is a veteran of «La Tissot». He admits to being almost 90 years old and to having enjoyed a generous pension for over 20 years!

I am a happy beneficiary of the Tissot-SSIH pension fund!, he says mischievously.

I ask him to explain why Tissot enjoys such a positive reputation amongst the inhabitants of Le Locle. It must be due not only to the quality of the company's social benefits, but also to certain of the Tissot family's public acts. It's true, he tells me. For example, Alfred Cortot was invited to give two concerts in Le Locle, one in the Casino and one in the Museum Halls, both very modest venues.

Just imagine, an internationally renowned musician!

But our neighbour, a charming young woman, replies: *Oh, him! The pianist who was always breaking his nails ... He had to interrupt the concert ... That really made us laugh!*

But Charles is undeterred. The Tissot family are also involved when Jeanne Gabrielle Tissot, herself a talented musician, organises the receptions in the Rue de L'Argillat. Her husband, Edouard-Louis, an art lover, is on friendly terms with the pianists Clara Haskil and Bela Siki, the latter an «honorary citizen» of Le Locle.

Monsieur Charles's neighbour, who has been listening closely to our conversation, breaks in: *It's like Mademoiselle Tissot, who, with her brother, set up the Foundation for Social Works and the pension fund; she wanted to contribute to the well-being of her collaborators. They were real bosses, my poor friend!*

The *dialogue* continues. A fresh anecdote is recounted: *In 1952, the Fabriques d'Assortiments, Zenith, Dixi, Aciera and Tissot got together to build workers' houses in the Quartier Neuf and the Quartier de l'Industrie.*

As Workshop Manager, Paul Tissot offered me a reasonable rent on a house built for the factory's middle managers. He said that the staff had to be made to feel happy with their lot so that they felt a part of the company and that, consequently, they had to have decent housing.

I am, alas, unable to reproduce the tone of voice in which my hosts recount their memories. In order to prolong our conversation, they all order a glass of Côtes du Rhône.

«A glass for everyone!»

For many years Madame Pierrette has been taking care of Tissot's elderly ex-employees. She's a kind woman. She organises excellent Christmas parties.

But Old Henri there will tell you about that!

So, let's listen to Henri: «*At the Christmas party of 1939, when we had all been mobilised, Mr. Paul Tissot visited the families of the Tissot employees who had been called up to give each of them a sumptuous box of victuals. And after the Armistice, we were all invited to the boss's home and given a franc for our demob!*

Along with many others, we served in the forces for 1,000 days. When we were first mobilised my wife had to make do with 3.95 francs a day to feed our two children. So, from time to time, I asked for a ten-day break to come and work at the factory and take some money home.

135

One of the ladies present comments: *You should remember that, between the wars, the average wage of these «good workers» was 1 franc 50 centimes, or, in other words, 144 francs every two weeks. We had six days' paid holiday, during which we went to the Lake of the Four Cantons by train ... What an expedition!*

Industrial Air Protection, Tissot, 1939-1945.

The collective memory awakened by my curious questions brings to the fore images of British Spitfires flying through the skies over Le Locle, the noise of warning sirens filling the night as Milan and Turin were bombed, the French laying down their arms at the local parish hall, the Germans who, in 1945, were evacuated from the sanatorium in Villers and moved to the Independent Church in Le Locle.

The staff at Tissot were part of the IAPF (Industrial Air Protection Force). In the photograph taken outside the factory you can see Marie Tissot and Yvonne Simon in their role as Good Samaritans.

Dr. Monot was the one who taught us how to use guns, how to wear gas masks, and various other things. At night, when the sirens went off, we raced to the factory, ready to defend it against all comers... our dear factory, our livelihood, you know!...

The Christmas holidays have a special place in the hearts of the factory employees gathered around me.

They talk about those friendly December mornings when Mademoiselle Mosimann and Ducommun used to visit the workshops dressed in their Salvation Army uniforms, singing Christmas carols, sometimes preceded by groups of schoolchildren forming little choirs.

The watchmakers particularly appreciate the breakfast from 7 a.m. to 8 a.m. on Christmas Eve.

Even Old Man Henchoz was willing to let us take that hour off. You know, we were at our workbenches for ten hours without a break!

137

The setters even used to treat themselves to a brief tour of the factory to visit the other workshops. The girls would exchange little presents … mandarins, chocolates, pistachio nuts.

Mademoiselle Jeanne-Alice speaks up very timidly.

Gentlemen, might I request a little silence, I ask, so that I can be sure of hearing all she has to say.

So, as well as dealing with orders, I received shipments, prepared them for various operations – either jewelling, which was carried out at Tissot, or nickel plating, which was sent out to a specialised workshop. When these operations had been completed, the pieces were sent back to me, and with the supplies I had kept on hold, I got everything ready to be sent to the Besbard company in Hauterive. That was a family concern run by a mother and her sons. The orders were often last-minute affairs. Mr. Maire brought everything over to them himself and went to collect the finished pieces, which ended up in the Final Verification Department. As well as the ébauches, *I also sent dials, hands, and cases.*

She interrupts her narrative, smiling sweetly; she is vaguely melancholic.

Hélène speaks up: *I chose to be a «régleues», thanks to the influence of my father, but I would have liked to be an accountant or an office worker… I love figures!… But my father said, and his word was final: «Setters are better paid».*

They have a less tiring job than office workers. And in fact even now, setters are in demand, hard to find. So I joined Tissot on 29th April 1940, with my colleague from Technicum, Rose Marie Perret; our boss sent us to work on the setting tests and on testing the new calibres.

Yvonne, in the Pochon shop window,
in Berne, circa 1947.

My brother Henri also went to work in the factory, after I'd started. We never talked about work at home. Our father didn't allow us to.

And now it is Yvonne's turn. *When my mother was widowed in the Spanish flu epidemic of 1918, she made me join Technicum. I cried every morning for a year on my way to work. But eventually I got used to it.*

In 1937, we were chosen, along with two colleagues, to go to German-speaking Switzerland to do «demonstrations» in the retailers' shop windows. We pretended to set our watches ... What I did most of all was to emphasise my slightly coquettish look, with nice hair and an embroidered dress... Even if my mother thought it was suspect!

It was impossible to concentrate, what with all the people who'd planted themselves outside the window to look at us! Sometimes we had a watchmaker with us sitting at his workbench. Look, I've kept this ring as a souvenir... it was a present from a retailer who was pleased with my «advertising' talents»!

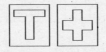

Why did I imagine that factory life would be nothing but work, discipline, rigour and filling the passing hours?

The people I've talked to here have proved me wrong.

But, sir, they really were the good old days!

What about our trip to Landi in 1939 – it was incredible, bosses who took their workers to the national exhibition! What a memory! And it was just at the start of the War!

While a sense of hierarchy can be readily discerned in every story told to me and while the codified relationships between bosses and subordinates and men and women which characterise these anecdotes are unquestionably linked to reality, the codes break down to a large degree in certain particular circumstances.

Zum 100 jährigen Jubiläum
bringt Tissot...

1853–1953

...eine ganz besondere Leistung: die
Tissot-Centenary, *die automatische Uhr,*
die Ihnen jeden Tag das Datum angibt.

Die *Tissot-Centenary* gibt Ihnen zeit Ihres Lebens nicht nur Stunde,
Minute und Sekunde, sondern auch noch das jeweilige Datum an, mit
einer Präzision, die Sie immer und immer wieder neu begeistern wird.
Diese neueste Schöpfung von *Tissot* — eine Jubiläumsleistung! —
ist stoßgesichert, wasserdicht, wissenschaftlich antimagnetisch und...
automatisch! Der neue, patentierte Tissot-Rotor zieht die Centenary
mit jeder Handbewegung auf — sicher, regelmäßig und absolut lautlos!
Rechnen Sie noch dazu, daß die *Tissot-Centenary* — wie alle Tissot-
Uhren! — auf den Tausendstel-Millimeter genau gearbeitet ist, und Sie
werden verstehen, warum jeder Tissot-Konzessionär Ihnen diese Uhr
— 18 Karat Gold! — mit besonderem Stolz zeigen
wird. Auf der ganzen Welt gelangt nur eine
beschränkte Anzahl numerierter *Tissot-Centenary* zum Verkauf. Preis Fr. 750.—.

Tissot
Centenary

1853–1953

100 Jahre im Dienste der Präzision

Nur bei den offiziellen Tissot-Vertretern erhältlich.
Die Uhrenfabrik CHS. TISSOT & FILS S.A., LE LOCLE, gibt Ihnen gerne die Adresse der nächsten Verkaufsstelle an.

Tissot *Centenary,* 1953.

I understand, in effect, that life in the Tissot factory, notably during the «Trente Glorieuses» the period of spectacular growth between 1945 and 1975 – was punctuated by festive get-togethers, family days out, fun-filled mountain walks, noisy *torrées* in summer or autumn, on the Sommartel Crest.

Yes, it's true, I remembered at that very moment, *Mr. Thiébaud invited me to the next* torrée *organised for all the factory staff!* I am intrigued by this strange word. My new friends explain: *A torrée is a kind of picnic!*

Let's be more precise. Imagine a primitive hearth composed of a few rocks set in a circle, in the centre of which are some crackling dead branches. From time to time, the armfuls of dry wood thrown on to the fire release a thick white smoke, spreading across the ground where it is whipped into tiny hurricanes by the swirling wind. Around this fire, happy men, women and children take great hunks of sausage roasting on the glowing embers.

Now it's Jean-Charles, a jovial 80-year-old, who evokes past times. He remembers:

I'll always recall a lady called Courvoisier, whom we sometimes employed in a workshop next to the office for special model repairs. She was about 60, small, thin and grey-haired, with parchment-like hands, a good-natured face and big eyes.

When the boss talked to her, she replied very quietly, still slightly bent over her machine, at most raising her head to look up with a serious expression at the man above her.

One day she was given a pretty gold watch to celebrate her 50 years of loyal service to the company. She wore it every day. She became a little less shy and showed off her watch with a faintly flirtatious air. Sometimes, on Saturday mornings, before everyone went home at a quarter past eleven (when everyone was putting their tools away and being slightly more free and easy because it was the end of the week), I went over to her. She chatted gently about factory life, about her children. She smiled and seemed happy... Dear Madame Courvoisier!

So many memories, so many anecdotes about times past, every one a chance to celebrate progress or to sing the praises of the «good old days».

Then, suddenly, everyone starts to talk at the same time.

Some people tell me that they have old photograph albums at home, others say that they still have the napkin with the menu for the centenary celebrations printed on it... And the bottle of white wine imbibed at the factory's 125th anniversary... They mention the gaily decorated train which took them to Schaffhausen in 1953, the one on which they

Centenary Train, Tissot, 1953.

travelled to Lucerne in 1978... the fresh buns they had for breakfast at 9 a.m....

Rose-Marie says emotionally: *Mademoiselle Tissot posed with me for a photo in front of the Rhine Falls! It's not every* patronne *who would do that for a little working girl who makes* ébauches*!*

I will be discreet concerning the confidences made to me about the flirtatious meetings and promises of marriage that were part and parcel of these occasions... not one name shall pass my lips!

«A marvellous journey» for the guests taken to Schaffhausen. There were even important people there, like Edmond Guinand, Neuchâtel State Councillor, and Maurice Vuille, Prefect of the Mountains, and Henri Jaquet, President of Le Locle Commune, and Jean Pellaton, Secretary of the Employers' Association.

It was the first time I'd ever been on a 'works outing' ... and what an outing it was! Who would have thought that the entire staff of a large factory could make the magnificent journey from Le Locle to Stein am Rhein in a single day, stop off at the Rhine Falls and come back home in such comfortable conditions!

They ask me: *Do you think that the anniversary of 2003 will be as marvellous as that? Do you know whether they're going to lay on an aeroplane? That's what we were thinking about on the train back, in 1953... Imagining the day when, instead of a train, people taking part in a race would climb into immense jet planes – maybe nuclear-powered ones – flying faster than the speed of sound over not just our tiny country, but vast oceans!*

I note how the 1978 commemoration of the foundation of Tissot was less festive, since it took place against the backdrop of economic instability and substantial structural problems. Members of staff were worried about losing their jobs; rumours about major financial dif-

146

ficulties abounded. Nevertheless, the luxurious nature of the celebrations laid on by the managing director momentarily took people's minds off the situation.

Do you remember, Henri? In September, sales agents and Tissot dealers came from the four continents to Le Locle ... to our little village, think of that! What organisation! What chaos!

And Mr. Pierre Aubert, our Federal Councillor, who placed a bouquet of roses in Marie Tissot's lap 'on his own behalf and on behalf of the Federal Council', he said, elegant man that he is!

And the 500 Swiss distributors invited to the Monteux Palace on the shores of Lake Léman. With a fanfare of trumpets and all the trappings. Long dresses and dinner jackets, huge baskets of flowers ... Yes, it's true, the reception hall was awash with lot of flowers.

And they still want to tell me about the Tissot Sports Club, about archery, rallying, inter-factory football tournaments, of competitions between teams from the Swiss company's subsidiaries and other teams from the watch industry, about ski races, orienteering events, judo, table tennis, volleyball ... skittles, boule, gymnastics ... even chess and cards.

You forgot to mention the pipe-smoking competition! That was really fun!

Shadows lengthen over the old hall. A deep nocturnal silence, broken only by the occasional barking of a dog and the muffled sound of the town, lulls me to sleep...

The finishing line, Villars, 1938.

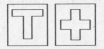

This morning I've put on a watchmaker's smock so that I can take a leisurely look around the loft.

You look like our Numa!

Perhaps I should adjust the height of the stool so that you're more comfortable?

Enough of this banter. My attention has already been attracted by a line of ochre-yellow cardboard boxes with shiny handles. They are stamped with the names of over one hundred of the world's countries.

What could they contain?

There is a grey envelope protruding from one of them. *Tissot Watch. Precision watch company. Le Locle & Geneva. Sales offices: Geneva, Rue de la Scie; Paris, Rue de Provence 7. Paris 1889, Member of the Jury; Paris 1900, Grand Prix.*

Just like the game shows on TV – a choice between two objects of research!

Either the history of the branches and sales offices, or the history of Tissot's participation in national, international and universal industrial exhibitions.

My choice is made for me by a sheet of headed notepaper listing all the medals won in these economic jousts.

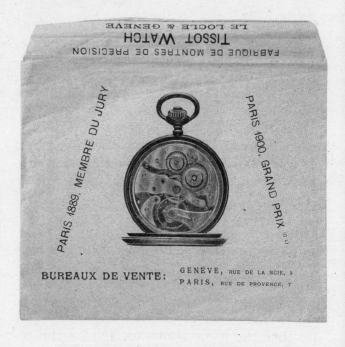

Tissot envelope, circa 1920.

SILVER MEDAL, PARIS, 1878. DIPLOMA OF HONOUR, ZURICH, 1888. GRAND PRIX AND GOLD MEDAL, ANTWERP, 1890. GOLD MEDAL, GENEVA, 1896. GRAND PRIX, PARIS, 1900. FIRST PRIZE FOR CHRONOMETERS AT THE NEUCHÂTEL OBSERVATORY COMPETITION AND FIRST PRIZE FOR MARINE CHRONOMETERS IN 1907. MEMBER OF THE JURY, CHICAGO, 1893; MEMBER OF THE JURY, PARIS, 1889.

Tissot headed paper, 1911.

I thus learn that, along with other representatives of the Swiss watch industry, Tissot took part in the Universal Exposition in Paris in 1878. Sixty-seven watches and five movements in silver frames, themselves set in cases, were

151

presented in a display case made in Le Locle.

Charles-Emile Tissot himself was a member of the jury or an exhibitor in other important exhibitions, including the one in Chicago in 1893, recorded in the annals and in the family photo album in the form of a group portrait of the members of the Swiss jury charged with its special mission by the Federal Council.

Charles-Emile Tissot, member of the Watch Jury, Universal Exhibition, Chicago, 1893.

That's why you will find a little grey-green volume in our modest factory library. Its author and title are: Charles-Emile Tissot, Special Report on the Horological Exhibition. Sine Loco, 1894. It is the official report delivered to the Federal Department of Foreign Affairs.

At that moment I am saved by my sense of tact from criticising the photograph. *This black pavilion with its lugubrious drapery is certainly in doubtful taste! What a shock to our eyes, which are more used to the designs of Sottsass, Vitra, Nouvel, Starck and Botta!*

Nevertheless, it was in places like these that the watchmakers spread their fame, sold their products, and built up loyalty amongst their clientele.

The next time you're here you must come and visit our stand at the Basel Trade Show and write your name in the Guest Book, suggests the generous guardian of the Tissot loft.

In the Swiss watchmakers' pavilion, Chicago, 1893.

Boîte No 22448

Facture de Jean Nardin fils

	G.	C.
Poids brut	18	68
Poids fini		
Déchets		72 40

Sav. or Cassine goutte
0,750 pendl ovale

Couronnes	avec la boîte	
Gravure		
Guillochis	partie	
Finissage de cuvette	poli	
Secret Bonggli		1 50
Glace		25
Etui	fr 208,20	
Finissage de boîte		2
Différence de façon		
Déchets		
Total		77 20

Exposition de Paris 1900

1 Avril 1900

RÉCAPITULATION

Coût de la boîte	77	20
Coût du mouvement	131	50
Prix de revient de la montre	208	70
Bénéfice de la montre		
Prix net de la montre		

Vendue à Sarah Bernhardt
à l'exposition de Paris
le 18 Mai 1900

Sold to Sarah Bernhardt … Paris, 1900.

The Guest Book? Show it to me, please.

I have always been fascinated by the autographs of men and women swept to the summit of celebrity by public interest or other fickle forces.

But before I get to see it, the «Living Memory of the Company» recites a list of celebrity Tissot customers since the 1880s. Good patriot that he is, he begins with the name of the Neuchâtel-born Federal Councillor Numa Droz, and continues with Albert Gertsch, Chancellor of the Swiss Consulate in Brazil, R. Ringier, Federal Chancellor, and Marc Rucher, Federal Councillor.

And he also mentions the great French actress Sarah Bernhardt.

When she visited the Universal Exposition in Paris on 18th May 1900, she chose a gold Tissot hunting watch to wear during her performances!

He thinks for a moment: *In 1921, we delivered a special watch, ordered by Queen Elisabeth of Belgium who was about to make an official visit to Brazil with her husband King Albert I. The hours on the dial were marked with the letters of the name «Elisabeth», embellished with diamonds, and the royal crown of Belgium replaced the missing figures.*

Only the memory of the salesman himself attests to the time when, in 1947, Joseph Holzer sold the South American singer Carmen Miranda a richly jewelled Tissot watch, part of a collection of 12 special pieces. There are also 12 black and white photographs on fine cardboard.

Carmen Miranda's choice in 1947.

We again have to rely on aural witnesses who report that, in 1949, His Royal Highness the Prince Bertil of Sweden wore a Tissot watch. However, my interlocutor tells me, *in this case, it has not been possible for us to find much in the way of supporting evidence. In fact, our watches are sold through retail shops. It's generally only later that we learn that one or other of our watches has been purchased by a maharajah or a similar VIP.*

But wait, I'll go and get you some eloquent press cuttings!

In effect, when, on 7ᵗʰ October 1953, Mr. Winthrop G. Brown, Minister of Commercial Affairs at the American Embassy in London, visited the Tissot factory in the company of Mr. A. Amez-Droz, President of the Swiss Chamber of Horology, an article about the official visit appeared in the press.

I am beginning to understand how advertisements and publicity have used celebrities to advantage. Two further examples of the phenomenon are provided by the June 1956 visit of H.R. Sawbridge, the Consul General of Great Britain in Geneva, and the Prefect of the Neuchâtel Mountains; and a visit of a dignitary from Lagos, Nigeria, in 1963.

Don't hurry … Take your time, says my interlocutor in a mysterious, somewhat suave tone of voice.

A certain 9th November 1960, at Le Locle.

The visit of the Monaco royal couple is recorded in the Tissot Guest Book in an entry for 9th November 1960, an entry which also includes the signatures of Max Petitpierre, the President of the Swiss Confederation, and his wife. Even if the beautiful Grace Kelly spent no more than 45 minutes in the Tissot factory, memories of her visit live on. The official programme has been carefully preserved. You can see the rapidly taken notes on protocol and the words of welcome pronounced by Edouard-Louis Tissot.

The *Feuille d'avis des Montagnes* newspaper did not miss the chance of reporting this extraordinary visit.

Yesterday, Le Locle gave the sovereigns of Monaco an enthusiastic welcome, which exceeded all expectations. Long before the time set for the arrival of the royal party, the inhabitants of our town, along with people from Berents, La Brévine and other villages in the district, had gathered along the route and, especially, around the Tissot factory, where there was a crowd of some 2,000 to 2,500 individuals… At two minutes past three, the sumptuous black limousines appeared at the bottom of the Rue des Tourelles and were greeted by cheering crowds…

Dressed in a simple beige woollen coat, the Princess sported a black fur toque which almost entirely covered her blonde hair. She wore neither a necklace, nor a bracelet, nor a watch!

At the end of their meeting, Edouard-Louis Tissot presented Princess Grace with a number of gifts intended for the children: a fine wrist-watch in rubies and gold (by Tissot, of course!) in a red presentation case for Caroline, and a large music box for Albert.

It was Pellaton who told me that the staff employed at the workbench had been ordered not to look the Princess in the eye, but to look at the floor instead.

Another press cutting features the snowy summit of Mount Titlis, which was visited by King Baudouin of Belgium and his wife in October 1989.

Could there be a more appropriate place to present a Tissot «Rock-Watch», cut from Alpine granite, to the royal visitors to the Swiss Alps?, exclaims my companion excitedly.

Walking back through the factory's lower storeys, I notice the offices of the Marketing Department covered in photographs of Grace Kelly, Princess of Monaco, the charming recipient of an immaculate bouquet of lilies of the valley.

I also notice the well-known outline of the Cervin, that emblem of the Swiss Alps, from whose cavernous depths was extracted an immense *Rockwatch* with red and yellow hands.

Tissot *Rockwatch* poster, 1986.

In the same corridor we run into a salesman who has been working for Tissot for almost 40 years. He tells us about some of the things he has heard on his professional travels around the world. He recalls that Elvis Presley wore a Tissot watch during his military service in Germany when he was a G.I.s. He also informs us that Nelson Mandela kept his Tissot watch during his 28 years of incarceration in a South African jail.

Again from Africa, a letter written by a missionary in 1953 contains a charming tale. Here it is:

By the way, I believe that this much-talked-of Tissot was the best watch for the Tropics. I have been here for five years without mishap, while the other Fathers who came here with me have seen their watches either attacked by the saline air, or by sweat, or by other such things. And yet, with the kind of work I do, Lord knows if my watch hasn't been through the wringer. It has fallen off my wrist, been dropped on to a concrete floor three times and never caused any problems. Unfortunately, at the beginning of the year, one of my young indigenous Brothers dropped it into a river. Adieu …

If you can spare a little more time, I'll show you a recent letter...

A few lines later, I see that today in the United Kingdom, Sir Edward Heath, the former Prime Minister, is proud to announce that he has been the owner of a Tissot watch since 1951.

I've always worn a Tissot watch when sailing the oceans, conducting orchestras and meeting world leaders. I am delighted with this historic timepiece.

I call for my loquacious guide, who, it seems, is familiar with this maze, a maze in which I feel completely lost, like Theseus in the Labyrinth.

What nonsense! I still know where I'm going!

Let's go back to Paris, if you want, for it is to Paris I shall return at the end of my sojourn in Neuchâtel.

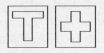

S omeone who used to be a travelling salesman for Tissot has agreed to see me. His first words are words of warning. *You know, I can't remember anything any more. It was more than 60 years ago! My memory's not what it was and, anyway, why should you be interested in my stories? My son and grandson work for Tissot. Go and talk to them!*

He nevertheless welcomes me to his home.

I ask him a few questions. We are sitting on a deep Neuchâtel-style sofa covered in rough material. The old man's eyes are slightly glazed. He is searching his memory.

He hasn't forgotten anything.

On the contrary, he is very precise. The French market was developed after the Universal Exposition in Paris in 1878. A Tissot outlet was set up in Rue Montmartre in the French capital in the period following.

When Tissot took part in the Lyons Trade Fair of 1917 to try and find new markets, the French ban on imported luxury goods was hindering the development of the outlet that had just been opened in Rue de Provence, Paris. The shop was later moved to Rue Saint-Lazare.

I take the opportunity to impart a fact of my own: *It was in the Rue François 1ᵉʳ in Paris, very close to the major jewellers, that, in the early 1990s, I was first able to admire the lovely creations of Longines, Omega and Tissot. Now there are 55 shops in Paris representing Tissot!*

He replies by painting a portrait of Paul Tissot, a vigilant and ambitious man, always ready to anticipate market demand. In 1930, he told his sales force: *We need to make a serious effort to reorganise, to bring in new ideas more attuned to the new situation. We need to make profits, otherwise, sooner or later, we'll have to put the key under the mat.*

Look! This is a very significant map of France!

The image that he shows me is set in a silver frame on the piano and surrounded by family portraits. An incongruous juxtaposition.

LE PLAN TISSOT
- (A) des modèles *choisis*
- (B) des produits *garantis*
- (C) des étalages *qui parlent*
- (D) une publicité *qui vend.*

Total... DES BÉNÉFICES!

Le plan Tissot : des idées *nouvelles* pour faire des bénéfices

Tissot Plan, 1934.

The map shows the rapid progression of the number of Tissot distributors in France. This increase demonstrates the degree to which the advertising and marketing plan of 1933 was in tune with the needs of the Swiss watch industry of the time. In January 1935, there were 84 distributors in France; in July of the same year there were 204.

I continue to study the document. My interlocutor becomes impatient. He has more to tell me. He explains how the approach to international markets was naturally organised within the framework of the SSIH, which sent travelling salespeople from the two bodies to the same centres of commerce.

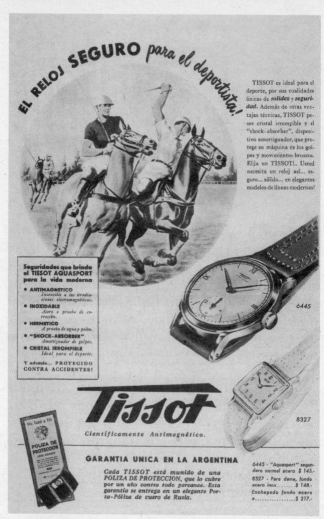

EL RELOJ SEGURO *para el deportista!*

TISSOT es ideal para el deporte, por sus cualidades únicas de *solidez* y *seguridad.* Además de otras ventajas técnicas, TISSOT posee cristal irrompible y el "shock-absorber", dispositivo amortiguador, que protege su máquina de los golpes y movimientos bruscos. Elija un TISSOT!.. Usted necesita un reloj así... seguro... sólido... en elegantes modelos de líneas modernas!

Seguridades que brinda el TISSOT AQUASPORT para la vida moderna

● **ANTIMAGNETICO**
   Insensible a las irradiaciones electromagnéticas.
● **INOXIDABLE**
   Acero a prueba de corrosión.
● **HERMETICO**
   A prueba de agua y polvo.
● **"SHOCK-ABSORBER"**
   Amortiguador de golpes.
● **CRISTAL IRROMPIBLE**
   Ideal para el deporte.

Y además... PROTEGIDO CONTRA ACCIDENTES!

6445

8327

Tissot

Científicamente Antimagnético.

POLIZA DE PROTECCION

GARANTIA UNICA EN LA ARGENTINA

Cada TISSOT está munido de una POLIZA DE PROTECCION, que lo cubre por un año contra todo percance. Esta garantía se entrega en un elegante Porta-Póliza de cuero de Rusia.

6445 - "Aquasport" segundero normal acero $ 145.-
8327 - Para dama, fondo acero inox.......$ 148.-
Enchapado fondo acero a.................$ 217.-

In the Buenos Aires daily, *La Prensa*, 1947.

In 1933, I signed an agreement with Paul Tissot according to the terms of which I would carry not only Omega, but also Tissot and Lemania in the territories I was responsible for. I travelled the length and breadth of Austria, Bulgaria, Denmark, Estonia, Finland, Greece, Hungary, Italy, Latvia, Lithuania, Norway, Poland, Romania, Russia, Sweden, Czechoslovakia, Turkey and Yugoslavia.

Tissot gave me a commission of 2½ per thousand on all the business done by the company in those countries.

In 1938, the travelling salesman Oscar Wolf was given the territories of Germany, South America, Central America, Mexico and the West Indies. In 1939, Jean Schaad was given Portugal.

You know, says my host, with a melancholy air, *our private lives were completely secondary. We were entirely dedicated to our brands. And time passes so quickly!*

Then he adds good-humouredly: *My first journeys by plane weren't automatically covered by the factory's insurance policy. Before each professional trip by air, you had to advise Winterthur so that they could cover the added risk with an additional clause. I never had any problems, except for the time I really saw the waves in the Bay of Hong Kong very close up.*

İsviçre birinci sınıf
Saatlarından

Herkese Elverişli

*Otomatik, kırılmaz, su geçmez, antimanyetik evsahları
bir arada modelleri tavsiyeye değer.*

Türkiye mümessilleri:

D. Galimini ve Ortrı   *Fazlı Balkan*

İstanbul   **İzmir**

In *İsviçre birinci sınıf*, Istanbul, circa 1950.

From the 1950s, Tissot accelerated the development of its sales policy and the organisation of its retail networks, notably by setting up subsidiaries and offices abroad. Certain agents, such as De Marchi in Italy and Holzer in South America, played an important role.

Let me tell you about an interesting experience De Marchi had.

When De Marchi carried Omega and Tissot products, he always started with the Omega samples.

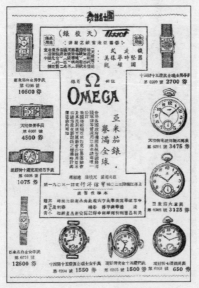

Tissot advertisement in Chinese, circa 1948.

When he got to the Tissots, the client was so tired that he hastily ordered a few pieces to go with the Omegas. From 1958 on, two teams of salesmen visited the client at different times. Mr. De Marchi maintained his figures for Omega, and considerably improved them for Tissot.

My host's son has joined us. He too is a devoted employee of Tissot. With a straight face, he points out: *Like all my colleagues, I dream of nothing but Tissot. We're all in the same boat.*

Electric sign, circa 1935.

But, unperturbed, his father continues with his story.

We often entertained our clients at Le Locle. We had some wonderful soirées, *the kind appropriate to promoting a convivial salesman-client rapport. There are many photo albums to prove it. We took them to see La Brévine. I remember that they found the smell of the manure from the large Neuchâtel farms that lined the route very picturesque*

It's true, I remark, *the loft of the Tissot factory contains a number of gifts the agents brought with them to give to the clients.*

As for the archives properly so called, they contain dozens of sales reports including analyses of the markets in Portugal, America, Japan, and many other countries.

I have learned that, these days, reports are sent by e-mail – does this mean that notes are no longer taken in the heat of the action?

During my stay in Berlin, we got news of General Hindenburg's victory over the Russians. I saw the city's inhabitants decorating their houses and hanging flags from the windows. However, in one shop where I had some business to do, there seemed to be a certain lack of enthusiasm and I was privy to a number of critical comments concerning the dispatch that had just been distributed throughout the city describing the victory.

The faithful salesman stands up.

Look, I've kept some of the fans that the Asian air companies used to give the passengers on their long-haul flights – fragile paper things on which we sometimes found the name of a brand of Swiss chocolate.

The housekeeper serves tea from a magnificent Russian samovar.

Black tea from the Steppes... Turkish Delight ...

Remembrance of things past... We have tasted the Proustian madeleine of a Swiss commercial traveller in the Slavic countries.

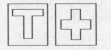

The working week is over.

The factory is closing its shutters, huge steel eyelids blanking out the ant-hill. It is impossible to pursue my inquiries within its walls.

Silence reigns there.

I hesitate in my choice of weekend excursion: the Watch Museum in Villers-Le-Lac, the Museum of Horology in Morteau, or the automata and music boxes in Ste-Croix? The «Horological Road» boasts dozens of interesting sites.

I hesitate yet longer in that I have been charmed by the huge music box at Neuchâtel station, an astonishing sight with its male and female dancers, who will twirl merrily for you if you put a coin in the polished wooden box.

Out of convenience, or because I am happily becoming acclimatised to the place, I decide to stay in Le Locle.

I suggest you visit the Château des Monts on the north side of the town.

How has my hostess, normally such a discreet woman, guessed what I am thinking about? She continues, anxious to give me some good-natured advice: *The Château houses a collection of watches and clocks from the region. You can also see an outstanding selection* (her choice of superlative!) *of foreign pieces. And it's a really lovely place!*

The «Château des Monts», Le Locle.

I struggle up the «Pillichody» path that I have been told about.

Ye gods! What a silly idea to build a villa in a bowl-shaped valley!

At the end of my exhausting ascent, I discover the Château des Monts housing the Horological Museum. The building is not far from the house where the watchmaker Daniel JeanRichard used to practise his art. The Château is set in an English-style garden bordered with ancient trees and an abundance of majestic meadow flowers. Two fashion engravings of pretty young Parisian ladies seem lost amongst so much calm, so much silence… so much peace.

The caretaker records my entry as soon as I walk up the steps between the two fierce and impassive bronze leopards on either side. He tells me somewhat ironically: *You'll find everything you need here. In the shop we sell Swiss chocolates and watches, books on watchmaking, Neuchâtel lace and bronze bell-caps! A fine choice of gifts to buy for your friends!*

A familiar figure here, Pierre, leads me through the rooms of the comfortable mansion. He tells me the history of this fine residence, built in the late 18th century, which the local people quickly began referring to as «The Château».

The first owner was Samuel DuBois, 'master small volume watchmaker', as opposed to 'large volume watchmaker', which means pieces for clock towers and, above all, clocks, he says, smiling faintly at my question.

From Samuel to Philippe, from Philippe to Frédéric-William, known as «DuBois of the Mounts», from Frédéric-William to Georges Ducommun, and from Georges to Hélène, the widow of Monsieur Nardin.

The commune acquired the house in 1954, making of this home of the great watchmakers of Le Locle a museum, a magnificent setting for collections from the School of Horology and for others assembled from important donations.

The building's interior preserves the typical character of the fine bourgeois homes of the Neuchâtel Mountains. Remember Madame de La Briche's descriptions!

Painted cabinet of a Neuchâtel clock.

Everything about the arrangement of the rooms, the inlaid flooring and the pine woodwork, conspires to create an ideal backdrop for floor clocks, Boulle marquetry wall-clocks, mantel clocks, Cartel clocks in golden bronze, Neuchâtel striking clocks, enamelled, polished, perforated and engraved watches and many other precious, imaginatively designed objects, including mirrors, perfume dispensers, mechanical song-birds and music boxes.

I can't get enough of this enchanted world.

Pierre shakes me from my dreamy fascination with these precious objects from centuries past. He tells me how the museums of the area have enriched their collections through purchases and, especially, through donations from manufacturers anxious to keep the region's watchmaking heritage alive. In this regard, he takes the opportunity of showing me the rooms which, next January, will be used for an exhibition of Tissot watches.

«1853–2003. Innovators by tradition». The contents of the display windows will be the concrete demonstration of the truth of the slogan launched throughout the world in 2002.

We are the beneficiaries of the generous aid of the company. Its dynamic management is going to completely refurbish both the room next to the library and the dining room. Our committee was delighted when it saw the new interior design which is to be the living witness of the 150th anniversary of Tissot in Le Locle. I am given an open invitation to visit the noble building whenever I desire!

I lean out of the many-paned window. Astonished by what I see, I turn around almost immediately to ask Pierre: *What on earth is that ... that elephant in the pavilion?*

He is amused by my amazement. Meanwhile, the master watchmaker is feeding the pachyderm with ... bronze balls.

That is a clepsydra, a faithful reproduction of the machine designed by the Arab scholar Al Jazarî in 1205.

In that manner I would, like a modern-day Phileas Fogg, have gone around the world in an hour!

Following the kind Museum archivist, I return to the bowels of the building, where the apprentice watchmaker-repairer is busy with his teacher. In the wide chest of drawers I discover a number of Tissot watches. Not the old pocket watches that I became familiar with the day before yesterday. No, these are wristwatches of an astonishingly modern design.

Like a commercial traveller preparing to show an impatient client the new collection inside his sample case, Pierre carefully displays a series of pieces that mark every single step in the evolution of Tissot's production of wristwatches since 1911.

Fabrique d'Horlogerie
CH. TISSOT FILS
Le Locle

Succ. de Chs~Emile Tissot

Maison Fondée en 1853

SPÉCIALITÉS : Montres soignées en tous genres de 8-20''' en platine, or, argent et métal. Chronographes-compteurs 19'''. Chronographes-compteurs 15''' bracelets. Montres ultra-plates, extra-soignées. Montres-bracelets simples et avec décors extra-riches en or et platine.

Prix de serie. à l'Observatoire de Neuchâtel
Primés aux diverses Expositions Universelles
Paris 1900 **Grand Prix** (C. L.)

Tissot advertisement, *Indicateur Davoine,*
La Chaux-de-Fonds, 1918.

Mechanically, he takes the pieces from their velvet-lined cases and polishes them with his shirtsleeve.

In so doing, he reproduces the gestures recommended to generations of travelling salesmen.

I do not lose the opportunity of telling him so.

After having cleaned the merchandise that has been handled, you will, if necessary, attach new labels and replace the items in their correct order.

The daily upkeep of the cleanliness and orderliness of the merchandise is obligatory; indeed, every week, and if possible, every day, you should check that everything is as it should be.

[*Instructions générales sur les voyages de commerce et en particulier sur ceux du commerce d'horlogerie*, Geneva, 1835.]

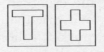

Allow me to be amazed once again.
You say that Tissot started producing wristwatches in 1911, but my researches suggest that this happened at a later date. I have read a lot about the influence of the First World War in the popularisation of this new type of timepiece.

It's true that the movements made by the Fabrique d'Ebauches de Fontainemelon, inserted into unlovely metal boxes, seem somewhat clumsy.

Look at this bracelet attached to the Lépine steel case, itself fitted with curved handles.

A strange object in search of an identity …

Pierre explains that the first wristwatches were designed with the fairer sex in mind. But after the War, men (not only soldiers, but also sportsmen and lovers of the outdoor life) were gradually won over.

181

Charles and Paul Tissot led the quest for new markets, a quest that had become all the more important after the events in Russia in 1917. The company's new orientation led them to abandon large pocket calibres and favour wristwatches. I note that these latter have bracelets in white or «mourning» satin, in moiré or nickel mesh.

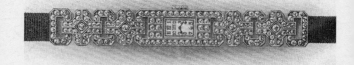

Tissot lady's wristwatch, 1928.

I repeat my question: *What became of the marvellous «top-of-the-range», pieces?*

Only the specialised jewel-inlaid watch collections still existed. There were increasingly fewer of those lovely complicated watches in the Tissot catalogue.

I conclude that, during the period, very high-quality Tissot watches at affordable prices became available to a large number of people.

I am also struck by the acuity with which, during the October Revolution, Charles analysed market demand in a letter to his brother Edouard, who was then in Basel:

Present demand in the watch market is increasingly concentrated on small pieces, indeed the smaller the better.

I hear the lobby bell.

A former president of the Château's committee walks into the building, greeting everyone in a hearty voice. No doubt the local tradition for conviviality, which I have already had occasion to mention, enables him to join our group without a hint of shyness. In fact, he instantly makes a contribution to our conversation.

When you're examining the wristwatches dating from the immediate post-WWI period, don't forget that, in 1918, Tissot transformed itself into a veritable manufactory. It began to make the ébauches for its movements on its own premises, and started to mass-produce them.

Our new companion goes to the library to look for a superb catalogue of lithographed colour photos, published by Tissot in 1929. In this lovely volume, I read of the influences of the artistic movements of the time (geometrical and stylised Art Deco and Art Nouveau designs), of fashion (wristwatches and hand-bag watches), of interior design (desk clocks with leather covers) and of sport (stopwatches).

How attractive these «Hermetic» watches are. I can think of one of my designer friends – something of a dandy, actually – who would be delighted to help make this timepiece – half pocket watch, half anniversary clock – fashionable again!

Leafing through the 1929 Tissot catalogue.

The watch can, if its owner so desires, be worn on the end of a cord. Sometimes there is a mirror set into the bottom of the presentation case. I notice how much care has been lavished on the decoration of these pieces: luxury leather, Chinese lacquer with inlaid eggshell and enamelwork. The silver cases all have leather presentation boxes.

And what do you think of this little round watch that you attach to your buttonhole? Original and convenient at the same time, isn't it? And this little tweezer-shaped watch, with symmetrical bright blue enamel inlay on a black enamel background?

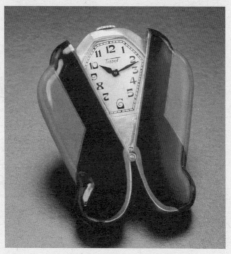

Tweezer watch, circa 1925.

The fashion for square watches gave way to a preference for round ones ... and vice-versa. *Basically, my grandfather's watch isn't as out-of-date as all that!*, I remark to myself.

The archivist from the museum is back with armfuls of boxes containing documents. She tells me that, amongst the private archives conserved in the Château, there is a very interesting collection belonging to a horology historian from Neuchâtel.

Thus, comfortably installed in the dining room in a deep, capacious armchair covered with Louis XIII-style *petit point* embroidery, I settle down to study a bundle of yellowed papers.

I begin to read.

It's a letter from Paul Tissot to Alfred Chapuis (the historian mentioned above), dated April 1937.

At the moment, the classic line is still popular and, curiously enough, is, in terms of round wristwatches for men, making a comeback in several countries. The reason for the continuing popularity of classic shapes is that the recent crisis demonstrated, in a peremptory fashion to say the least, that retailers whose watches were too extravagant managed to sell them for a short while, but were unable to sell them for a long time, a phenomenon which gave rise to all the usual difficulties of loss of interest, build-up of stock and cash-flow problems.

However, underlying everything is the question of 'quality', a question which is central. Enormous progress has been made in this field. By drastically reducing the size and thickness of watches, fashion has made the study of the relative proportions of different components, the mathematical precision of which is vital in watchmaking, particularly important.

I had never imagined that there was a link between technical constraints and aesthetic appearance.

I also discover that these same constraints are, in some places, defined by commercial obligations, the validity of which is accepted by all.

Pierre extracts from his presentation case an elegant wristwatch whose dial features a kind of double brand «Tissot-Omega Watch Co». For a fleeting moment I am nonplussed.

Undeterred, I grab my notebook. I remember having sketched out a precise «genealogy».

In 1930, Tissot and Omega's respective Boards of Trustees signed an agreement recognising their common interest in both the commercial and industrial fields. The origins of the agreement went back to 1925. The official act of 1930 marked the inception of the SSIH, or *Société Suisse pour l'Industrie Horlogère* (Swiss Society for the Horology Industry). The company's headquarters were located in Geneva. From that moment, it seemed clear that production would be organised on the basis of the SSIH agreement, that, effectively, Tissot and Omega would share a common production plan. Henceforth, Tissot was to produce certain calibres under the Omega brand and vice-versa. And conjointly.

Twin brand: *Omega Watch Co Tissot*, circa 1935.

It is also through this arrangement that some Tissot calibres were made by Lemania, the former President points out.

In effect, I remember what Mr. Jean-Charles told me a few days ago in the Place du Marché:

This is what Paul Tissot said. I was still a young man at the time! «In Bienne, we have just taken the decision to design and produce a new automatic calibre at Le Locle for the SSIH (Omega + Tissot + Lemania, you remember?).

Mr. Henchoz will direct and advise you in this task. So, what do you think?

That's why I spent another year in Le Locle, to work on the development of the 28.5 calibre with a rotor with an axial support piece. In fact, you can see one of the prototypes at the Museum at the Château des Monts.

I examine the automatic movement, amusing myself with the oscillating mass for a while... Perhaps I've never entirely grown up!

You have in your hands one of Tissot's pioneering works.

Tissot advertisement, 1933.

How, why?

After having designed and produced watches with anti-magnetic movements and then distributed them all over the world starting in 1933, Tissot was able to dominate the automatic watch market for a substantial period of time. There was a profusion of watches of this kind in the decade between 1945 and 1955 and you can still find them in the catalogue.

From his exposé, I remember that Paul Tissot ordered a study from a New York agency, which confirmed that a large percentage of the watches left with the repairer were magnetised. In 1933, a programme of systematic studies on the causes and consequences of magnetisation was launched in Le Locle. The Tissot anti-magnetic watch, the first of its kind to be introduced on to the market, was rapidly imitated by other brands.

Anti-magnetic Tissot watch, circa 1940.

Wir haben von einer der weltbekanntesten Publizitäts-Agenturen der Firma Thompson in New York eine Untersuchung bezw. Markt-Analyse s. Zt vornehmen lassen, um feststellen zu können, ob die antimagnetische Tissot-Uhr seitens der Kundschafts als nötig erachtet wurde.

Please, sir, slow down so that I can take some more notes! I think that it is his enthusiasm, the kind of enthusiasm characteristic of technicians, who are proud of their work, which makes him so voluble.

Tissot automatic movement, 1944.

At your ease, Sir Scribe!

He starts to read, with finesse: *A woman's forgetfulness when it comes to winding her watch is a delightful foible which characterises the kind of adorable feminine fantasy which sits ill with this daily discipline! That is why watchmakers have put their minds to furnishing her with an advantage which was, for many years, the exclusive privilege of men – the automatic watch!*

Is he taking me for a credulous neophyte?

He shows me a small Tissot automatic lady's watch with a date function. Then, displaying a certain compassion in regard to my limited knowledge, he hands me an article from an illustrated magazine dated April 1952. He says: *In a sense, this is the Navigator's birth certificate. Read it, you'll understand why.*

A large watch company has just started mass-producing a wristwatch which rapidly tells its owner what time it is anywhere in the world. Thus, to meet the demands of progress, our industry has made available to the many a product designed and made by a few inventors working alone in their ateliers.

Tissot *Navigator*, 1953.

Tissot worldwide, 1951.

*We wish these new ambassadors of the ingenuity
and skill of Swiss workmanship the best of luck.*

The article is about the «Tissot Automatic
Navigator», the fruit of a project directed by
Louis-Edouard Tissot, Marie and Paul's cou-
sin, who had returned from Argentina (where
he ran an electricity company) when Paul died
in 1951.

At that moment, Pierre discreetly points out
a beautiful gold watch, whose dial seems to me
to be rather complicated: *The Navigator is an
automatic watch which gives the time all over the
world; it is part of the collection which marked*

Tissot's centenary and, later, its 125ᵗʰ anniversary.
They designed several new watches for each celebra-
tion. For the 100ᵗʰ anniversary it was easy. They
created an automatic watch for the occasion and cal-
led it the «Centenary».

I had not thought about it before, but it is
amusing to consider the names given to parti-
cular models: The *Tissot*, The *Navigator*, The
Centenary, The *PR516*, The *PR100*, The *Classic
Prince*, The *Bellflower*, The *T-Win*, The *T-Touch*.
The usage corresponds to the way in which
local people refer to members of the family:
«The Marie», «The Paul» … but also «The Fat
Bloke» or «The Flea»!

I continue to leaf through the old catalogues. I discover that the sports watches in the
Tissot Camping collection, created in 1938,
feature all the modern technical characteristics – they are waterproof, dust-proof, anti-
magnetic, with unbreakable glass, stainless
steel case.
It's true, I say to myself, *I've never really thought
about the traumas making up the life of a watch!*
Now, how often does your faithful watch have
to struggle against life's vicissitudes?
Shock-resistant, anti-magnetic, dust-proof,
self-lubricating, water-resistant, accurate – and
precise …

My little glossary is gradually filling up with new terms. I get the impression that it is a kind of tiny metaphor for the accelerating rate of technological universal innovation over the last hundred years and more!

Leafing through the pages
of Tissot's catalogue for 1938.

My companions amuse themselves by recounting a hilarious anecdote that has done the rounds in the Tissot factory. They tell me that the workshop manager, who had been given a watch to repair, still laughs about it to this day. It's a simple story of a watch belonging to a farmer. Sadly, the man's cow had swallowed the precious instrument. But in spite of its unfortunate transit, the valiant «Tissot automatic» is as good as new!

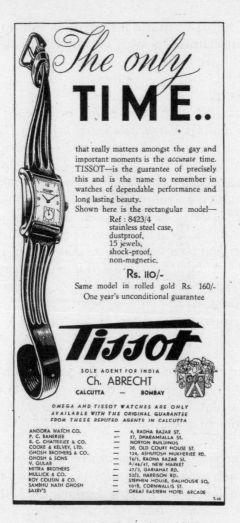

The only
TIME..

that really matters amongst the gay and important moments is the *accurate* time. TISSOT—is the guarantee of precisely this and is the name to remember in watches of dependable performance and long lasting beauty.

Shown here is the rectangular model—
Ref : 8423/4
stainless steel case,
dustproof,
15 jewels,
shock-proof,
non-magnetic,

Rs. 110/-

Same model in rolled gold Rs. 160/-
One year's unconditional guarantee

Tissot

SOLE AGENT FOR INDIA
Ch. ABRECHT
CALCUTTA — BOMBAY

OMEGA AND TISSOT WATCHES ARE ONLY AVAILABLE WITH THE ORIGINAL GUARANTEE FROM THESE REPUTED AGENTS IN CALCUTTA

ANGORA WATCH CO.	—	4, RADHA BAZAR ST.
P. C. BANERJEE	—	37, DHARAMTALLA ST.
R. C. CHATTERJEE & CO.	—	NORTON BUILDINGS
COOKE & KELVEY, LTD.	—	20, OLD COURT HOUSE ST.
GHOSH BROTHERS & CO.	—	124, ASHUTOSH MUKHERJEE RD.
GHOSH & SONS	—	16/1, RADHA BAZAR ST.
V. GULAB	—	8/46/47, NEW MARKET
MITTRA BROTHERS	—	47/3, GARIAHAT RD.
MULLICK & CO.	—	52/2, HARRISON RD.
ROY COUSIN & CO.	—	STEPHEN HOUSE, DALHOUSIE SQ.
SAMBHU NATH GHOSH	—	101B, CORNWALLIS ST.
SAXBY'S	—	GREAT EASTERN HOTEL ARCADE

T.10

ssot, *The Only Time*, circa 1950.

But let us examine a few other examples of the unscrupulous uses to which Tissot timepieces have been put.

Ladies and gentlemen, admit to your misdeeds!

I was washing my hands when my good old Tissot watch that I'd bought two years earlier in Calcutta fell from my wrist. Initially, it fell 20 feet, then a further 18 feet, landing on the edge of the piston cooler which was full of water and potassium bichromate at a constant temperature of 70°C, before disappearing into it. It stayed there for a week and could only be rescued when we had arrived in Colombo and the engines had been turned off so that the water could cool down. I washed it, rubbed it with an old cloth, and then rewound it. It started to go again and hasn't stopped since it had the adventure

[A.K. Banerji, mechanic on board the MV Isipingo, 1956].

Read this dispatch, I think you'll find it amusing. Quite what does it demonstrate? The progress of kitchen technology or the waterproof qualities of a Swiss watch?

He apparently left the watch in his pyjama pocket and, not realising the watch was in the pocket, I washed the pyjamas in my washing-machine, then rinsed and spin-dried them. I only discovered the watch as I was folding them and I thought I had rui-

ned it. However, it is going as well as it ever did. The only thing we had to buy was a new strap. Congratulations on making such a good watch. Yours faithfully, A. Henderson

[A. Henderson, North Shields, England, 15th December 1967].

The only one of my personal possessions that survived when my ship, the HMS Repulse, *was sunk by the Japanese on the same day as the* Prince of Wales, *9ʰ December 1941, in the China Sea, was my Tissot Nº 842.691. I had it on when I jumped overboard and when we were rescued by HMS* Electra *after splashing around for half an hour in an oil slick*

[Dr. S.G. Hamilton, Lieutenant-Colonel, Doctor RNVR, Surrey, England, undated].

The factory's correspondence registers are bulging with dozens of letters in the same style, some of them funny, others dramatic, says Pierre who, I have often noticed, enjoys the confidences of the guardian of the keys of the Tissot loft.

He adds: *It's a kind of indirect advertising, true stories like that one, which are very efficient, as word of mouth always is.*

In fact, the true stories crammed into the correspondence files constitute the chapters of an authentic novel in which reality is sometimes stranger than fiction.

You still have a little time before the Museum closes, so why don't you have a look at this box full of old copies of the «Tissot News». It's Tissot's external PR organ and it has been published since 1956. You can read about the major events in the history of the company and browse through anecdotes which give an insight into company life, from 1956 to 1970. Good luck!

Tissot advertisements published in *Life*, 1947.

Good people, you are about to hear a number of voices that bear witness to the deserved renown of Tissot watches!

For I have courageously accumulated reams of notes.

The resistance and reliability of Tissot watches are first demonstrated in an Atlantic crossing of 1923 (Alain Gerbault), and then in a series of speleological explorations (Robert de Joly, 21st September 1949), during a Danish Arctic expedition to Peary Land (1950), in treks across the Sahara (M. Haubensack, Trans-African Trek, 1959–1960), in expeditions to the deserts of Egypt and the Near East (M. Thiébaud, geologist), in other expeditions to the territory of Patagonia (Arnold Heim) and to the mountains of Peru (C.G. Villanueva, 1957), in car races (Harry Zweifel, 1958) and in a tour of Africa by bicycle (M. Claude, 1954).

- *In Australia, shark hunters are national heroes. The most famous of them, Ben Cropp, author of several books on deep-sea fishing, uses a PR516 when he embarks on his risky dives.*

- *The «Tallest Tissot Watch in the World» is the T12, which has conquered Everest. It's one of the most popular timepieces amongst mountaineers.*

- *Japan's Dr Takemi will consider buying a watch only after having examined it with a stethoscope. After applying the procedure to several different Tissot models, he plumps for the Seastar 7 whose crystalline «tick-tock» reflects a robust state of health.*

- *In Vietnam, helicopter pilot D.-F. Janik would like to thank Tissot for having saved him from a serious wrist injury. While helping to save a pilot whose plane had just been downed by the Viet Cong, his left wrist was hit by a bullet, which went through the bracelet – which, however, took the sting out of the experience – and lodged against the bone. In spite of this terrible shock, the watch is still in perfect working order.*

I have noticed in the course of my research that the medals won in industrial exhibitions and the market bulletins published by chronometric observatories were an important source of publicity at the beginning of the 20th century. They also expressed the precision and superior quality of Swiss timepieces the world over.

So Tissot patented watches at the Neuchâtel Observatory, their close scientific partner?

Pierre stops winding up the clocks which surround us and nods in acquiescence. He puts down his heavy bunch of keys and takes several bound volumes from the library shelves, reports written by the director of the Observatory for the authorities of the canton.

Tissot's first chronometric success dates from 1884 when the company won the first prize in the Chronometer Class B category.

He reads out loud, grandiloquently modulating the timbre of his voice. I am impressed by his hitherto hidden talents! *The first prize was won by N° 4 in the table, in other words by the anchor chronometer N° 65693 by Mr. Ch.-F. Tissot & Sons of Le Locle, which perfectly fulfils all the conditions stipulated for this category. This piece, as well as the following one, was set by Mr. Borgstedt at Le Locle.*

Without thinking, I applaud!

In 1908, Tissot repeated its success by winning the prize for producers and the setter category prize awarded to Mr. Perret, which put Tissot's watches out in front of those of Paul-David Nardin, Paul Ditisheim, Georges Favre-Jacot (Zenith) and Longines: *In fact, the elite of the watchmaking industry, as well as the elite of Neuchâtel setters, including Charles Rosat, Henri Rosat and Henri Gerber, Auguste Bourquin...*

But, still on the subject of advertising, Pierre, are the graphic artists working on Tissot's image today the descendants of a long tradition?

Of course, he contents himself with replying, as if the thing were so obvious that all other comment would be superfluous.

In fact, a number of questions come to mind – what are the complex visual sources of the sales catalogues and manuals now compressed on to this wafer-thin CD that I hold in my hand?

To find out, I shall probably have to go back to the factory where I saw a number of folders tied with ribbons in which, I would guess, are to be found layouts for adverts from the 1960s.

Perhaps I will meet other guides as well.

Be seeing you, then! Pierre says. He takes his leave of me by the big wrought-iron gate with its gilt spikes at the entrance to the Château park.

Till next time!, I reply, proud finally to be able to speak like the natives.

The day has been long and rich in new facts.

Aspects of the *T-Collection*, 1999.

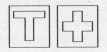

I t's early in the morning and the mist is rising slowly above the town of Le Locle.

Sitting in the only chair in a tiny hairdresser's salon, I consider a series of adverts cut out of various illustrated magazines. Someone has stuck them to the wall with large drawing-pins.

I am temporarily distracted by the chatter of a mynah bird.

But my thoughts return to the subject of Tissot…

Tissot *Diacolor* from the 1950s.

I have noticed that printed advertisements for watches dating from before 1920 are something of a rarity. However, I know that advertising was already a major industry in America. In my childhood, magazines like *Jours de France*, *Connaissance des Arts* and *Plaisirs de France* published – especially in their Christmas issues – lovely pages, adorned with elegant characters, vaunting the merits of quality Swiss watches.

In cinemas now … Tissot *Diacolor* from the 1950s.

Go and look for Tissot's close neighbours in Rue de Beau-Site … former Sales Directors – they'll be able to explain their policies. They'll be happy to see you, for sure, claims my Swiss Virgil, to whom I have confided my thoughts of the moment to feed some satisfaction into his hungry, scarcely hidden curiosity.

I have no difficulty in finding the first of the two directors I have been told about. He is sitting in a peaceful garden, under the generous shade of some old trees. The sweet odour of the season's last peonies, of the big orange poppies and blue lupins wafts gently on the air. «The neighbour» lifts his head to look at the sky. He follows the smoke curling from the fire which consumes the fruits of his weeding exploits.

A little later, the absinthe fountain dispenses two large glasses of cool, slightly coloured water. A lump of sugar slowly dissolves on the openwork spoon.

The odour is delicious … is it because we are close to discovering the secrets of the Green Fairy?

We don't do any advertising and we only visit our Swiss clients when we find the time between trips abroad.

Tissot's efforts in the field of advertising were held back by the kind of direct contact travelling salesmen (often the boss himself!) had with their clients. This special relationship was supported in business correspondence with headed notepaper abundantly illustrated with the medals garnered from various industrial exhibitions. The personal relationship engendered by these links was more important than any advertising campaign.

After 1917, with the quest for new markets becoming essential, Tissot regularly placed advertisements in magazines and newspapers. Publicity became a real subject for consideration from 1925 and this reflection led to the development of an innovative promotional tool using all the resources of advertising science.

Please bear this in mind. It's important – the Le Locle company's position in national and international markets was determined in 1933 with the adoption of the Tissot Plan.

He hands me a dark-coloured catalogue, featuring only the stylised signature of Paul Tissot on the cover, its slightly embossed pages held together by a garnet silk cord. I cast my eye over certain passages and am surprised by the modernity of the approach.

There is, therefore, next to the major brands, a niche to exploit for a small, mid-priced collection of watches including a few perfectly designed models guaranteeing the company a large turnover without investing too much capital, and marketed using a scientific advertising method. That is Tissot's niche.

Out loud, I observe: *Didn't this trace out Tissot's entire destiny for the decades to come?*

The old man smiles. I have identified one of Tissot's strong points: the precocity of their marketing strategies.

– *Not only were we ahead of our time in terms of advertising, in terms of how we presented our products in display windows or on posters or in ads in the press, but we were also pioneers in industrial terms.*

La buna ura de sac de precisiun
cun cassetta solida

– *Could you explain that?*
– *I wouldn't be able to. But I'll introduce you to a technician who can tell you about the industrial history of the Tissot manufactory – the adoption of the single calibre, the rationalisation of production methods, the first plastic watch, the technological prowess of the present day...*

It's true, I've already realised that the industry is subject to a constant tension between production constraints and commercial needs, two arrhythmic tensions intimately linked to the two sectors.

Tissot Lady's Calibre 15.3, 1947.

The opposing characteristics of sales (fluidity and versatility) and production (massiveness and permanency) create friction between, on the one hand, design and production lead times which are always too long and, on the other, pressure exerted by market demand.

*This last is a real constraint; it dictates innova-
tion in calibres and models, it governs stock flows,
and decides the commercial fate of collections. Our
entire marketing strategy is dependent on it. It's a
real school of anticipation and diplomacy!*

I have already seen, in the lively debates that
developed during the course of a meal shared
by former employees of the Tissot watch factory, that this is a subject which is bound
constantly to provoke over-zealous comments.
The salesmen cultivate a sense of superiority
from which the technicians defend themselves
with tenacious *bonhomie.*

But is the domination of the Sales
Department over the domain of the technicians real or imagined?

Why do the technicians feel that they are not
sufficiently valued compared to salespeople
whose reputation is heightened by the prestige
attached to their function?

Whenever the technicians believe that their
opinions are not taken seriously enough or
when a new product turns out to be a failure,
the sales force's strategy comes in for some
heavy criticism; and when other difficulties
arise and put the success of a collection in
doubt, the finger is pointed at the technical
departments.

It requires a certain skill to strike a balance between the naturally different mentalities of a salesman – a deft tactician – and a technician – a craftsman attached to his art. .

But there is also a concrete difference, which one can see at the structural level, in the salary scale, for example, or in terms of who gets promoted, and of who sits on the company's various councils and commissions.

– My dear sir, your analysis is very pertinent for a beginner!

Permit me to be proud of the progress I have made in the subject of horological structures... and mental attitudes!

The second neighbour presents himself.

He too is wearing the uniform of the amateur gardener. Under his arm he has a small grey box with an old leather belt tied around it.

I think about my bedtime reading sessions: *The watchmaker often has a little garden to tend, a few hens and rabbits to feed... The watchmaker of past times often preferred to spend his Mondays in the forest picking mushrooms, the famous morels which I had for supper.*

The second neighbour also uses possessive pronouns when talking about the activities of the company.

Our first real publicity was generated by our participation in various industrial exhibitions in the 19th century, then through trade journals, and later at the Basel Show in 1931.

At this time, the salesman's task was made easier by the availability of a good deal of sales material, including illustrated catalogues of cost-price models and brochures full of adverts which were to be published in the newspapers.

Sonderegger Chalet in Mürren, circa 1948.

«Just imagine! Tissot's first salaried travelling salesman – Jean Schaad – was hired only in 1924. He was joined two years later by Jean Simon. In 1957 it was Schaad's son who, upon the request of Marie Tissot took over from his deceased father. She it was who from 1916 onwards was in charge of the finances and day-to-day running of the business. The Swiss distributors of the brand showed every trust in her decision, And justly so, since Mr Schaad is still active even today!»

Marie Tissot, sometimes nicknamed «The Empress» due to her strict manner, was a fearsome character in the company. She had been responsible for the firm's finances since 1916.

Having adopted the theory that the public attributes a higher value to a watch made by a well-known company than to one made by a more obscure firm, Tissot developed a twin-pronged marketing strategy designed both to make its products known and to provide its sales force with all that was needed to ensure its success.

Romer shop window in Baden, circa 1940.

From reading a detailed and very precise press article, I come to understand how the advertisements were designed with those two goals in mind.

In 1933, Tissot took the entirely original step of providing its dealers, free of charge, with a sales material package (including stands, shop window signs, pedestals, display units and various pieces of decor), and a catalogue containing all the sales arguments that could possibly be of use to a retailer of Tissot watches.

My companion opens the box he has brought with him.

The advertising material also includes dealer logos, and photographs and pamphlets destined for use in press campaigns.

He reveals the contents – mostly stands packed one on top of the other – and shows me a brass plaque with a black enamel background against which is written in gold letters the name Tissot. He shows me another plaque – in the shape of a lozenge this time – with an identical function: to identify the retailer as an official Tissot dealer.

It was our job to tell them to reserve the best spot in their display windows for the Tissot collection and to make sure they featured the official Tissot dealer sign!

My narrators continue their story, taking it in turns, swinging to and fro like the pendulum of a Neuchâtel clock.

But you can't imagine the scandal when, in 1933, Paul Tissot introduced an unconditional one-year guarantee for all Tissot watches. He had to abandon the idea due to pressure exerted by the Zentral Verband Schweizerischer Uhrmacher.

Nowadays, salespeople provide customers with a two-year certificate of guarantee for all Tissot watches. That's a tangible sign of the progress made by modern watchmakers in terms of reliability.

Tissot display, circa 1940.

After Sales, a complementary part of the training of all sales personnel, is a crucial aspect of company organisation. Indeed, the reputation of the company as a whole depends on it.

Historically, Tissot's management has always been very concerned with developing the best communication strategy possible – ensuring that display windows are attractive and placing advertisements which are not only good to look at, but effective too!

It is at this point that I realise that, up until 1990, Tissot watches had been sold exclusively by retail dealers. It was only ten years ago that members of the public began noticing them in department stores.

Between 1942 and 1945, our Swiss turnover benefited from the purchasing power of Polish refugees living in the country; between 1945 and 1948, the G.I.s spent some time in Switzerland before returning to the U.S.; and, starting in 1950, temporary residents from Italy constituted a faithful clientele for a number of years.

I'm quite a fan of polls. That's why I find it interesting that, in 1952, just such a poll revealed that Tissot was the second most well-known watch company in Switzerland after Omega.

The Swiss market has become an important and demanding client for the Le Locle-based company. Recent polls have confirmed this to be true. That is why we have adopted an appropriate slogan, which perhaps you have seen: «Tissot – Switzerland's favourite watch».

FABRIQUE D'HORLOGERIE CHS TISSOT & FILS S. A. LE LOCLE - SWITZERLAND   SEPT. 1962 - II

Engagement presents, wedding presents, first communion presents, graduation presents, birthday presents ...

Is it possible that every family in Switzerland owns at least one Tissot watch? If not, we at least know that a majority of present and former Federal Councillors have one.

When you're giving a Swiss watch, give the best – Tissot.

A memory flashes through my mind. How could I have forgotten that my godfather gave me a watch for my first communion – a Tissot «Stylist», so slender that it seemed to me to be overly fragile? Where did I leave it, ungrateful person that I am?

But information continues to arrive, like a telex print-out.

As if wearing seven-league boots, we travel effortlessly through the decades.

In the late 1970s, our aim was to sell at least 3 million Tissots per year worldwide and thus organise a successful rearguard action against the competition from Japan which was jostling and manhandling the ancient status quo of the Swiss watchmaking industry.

In the long term, Tissot's goal was to dominate the mid-sector of the watch market. Indeed, according to the slogan we used at the time, Tissot gave you «more watch for your money».

The words of François Thiébaud flit into my memory: *For a long time, Tissot was a brand well known to watch makers but not to the end user. We have made it more accessible to customers. After the crisis, an economic improvement around 1986 was followed in 1996 by the beginning of a real burst of growth, which has not yet slowed down.*

Thiébaud, the company's President, reels off a few more figures. Tissot's products are distributed through a network of some 15,000 points of sale around the world and 520 shops in Switzerland. The management are happy with the figures for 2002, even though they are extremely vigilant about market variations. *We are millionaires twice over in watches!*

As reddish streaks colour the sky, the second neighbour tells me more about the Basel Fair. An occasional visitor to such trade shows, I am curious to learn a few details about what goes on backstage, a subject I had never really considered before.

In 1959, in the watch section of the Swiss Samples Fair in Basel, the new Tissot stand attracted a great deal of attention.
Of a completely new, absolutely original design, it marked a profound change in the architectural style of watch company stands at the Basel show. The

work of Tissot's designer, the light-filled, spacious, very panoramic stand was set around a cabin-cum-sitting room with burnt mahogany sliding doors.

The Basel Fair is a cardinal event which focuses efforts in creation and innovation. The Fair is used to introduce new products to the press and to dealers, whose orders are taken during a ten-day period of intense activity.

It was sometimes impossible for us to get away for so much as five minutes..., he says with a knowing air. *I've kept a telex from 1977 which says: 'First indications from the Basel Fair – Tissot sales excellent. Total 1976 turnover bettered in just five days. Very positive reaction to new gold and quartz wristwatches. Positive atmosphere in regard to the brand. The Tissot Switzerland team'.*

Replace 1977 with 2001 or 2002 and the sales are still excellent.

I admire photographs of the modern stand – a white cross against a bright red background and a shiny black «T». *Symbols both of our quality and of our duty: always do better, always to do more,* François Thiébaud has told me. *The Swiss flag which makes up part of our logo has at its heart a white cross, which for me represents the «plus» sign, a dynamic symbol, which stands for a quest for quality that should never be forgotten ... I wish to make it a guiding principle.*

After demonstrating the sharpness of his memory by outlining the exact progression of the turnover figures achieved over the last 35 years and more, my interlocutor completely changes the subject.

I'm a collector of old cinema projectors. Allow me to invite you to a little private viewing. We'll organise it to coincide with our aperitifs.

I'm sure it will interest you!

What is the relationship between watchmaking and cinema?

Well, they do both include gears and temporal sequences!

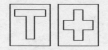

We spend the evening watching a series of short films which give the history of the company a new rhythm and relief. Some are funny, some romantic, some are sharp and others irritating. They all, however, offer food for thought.

I would like to describe the contents of the session for you.

But I have to say that there is no popcorn or ice-cream during the intermission! And that I haven't stopped taking notes …

Filmed in 1954, «Depuis cent ans, toujours présent» (One Hundred Years of Activity) features animated dolls presenting Tissot watches old and new and a number of major inventions which have marked the history of the measurement of time.

Depuis cent ans, toujours présent.

In 1959, Tissot made direct use of the cinema for advertising purposes – one of the company's timepieces appears in close-up in the British comedy «The Ladykillers». The watch is used by the actor Alec Guinness to precision-time a hold-up. They always said the English had a dry sense of humour!

«When Midnight Strikes» is a playful introduction to the first collection of the 1960s, while the seventh Tissot advertising film was used to promote the «Visodate Automatic» watch.

The projectionist interrupts the show and tells me that, *In 1962, an original production was screened simultaneously in some 180 Swiss cinemas. The film, «Simpler and More Accurate», was shown in the country's cities and large towns. It explained the advantages of Tissot's «single calibre» – you know, the basic calibre with four variants.*

Both 16mm and 35mm films are projected. In no particular order, we see the *PR516, Sideral, Seven,* the *PR518, Stylist.* The films have been screened all over Europe.

– But what is the real impact of these films, films designed to promote both products and sales? Isn't it true to say that it is a very difficult task to gauge the true scale of their influence?

– I can assure you that the effect is obvious. In 1972, the TV ad that we just saw played a vital part in the success of the Tissot Sideral. In February and March of that year, after the advert had been shown, sales increased by 31% and 39% respectively.

Under the cardboard box containing reels of film, there's another one full of videos... *Rock-Watch... Two Timer... PR100... Autoquartz... T Touch...*

A friendly tip – the adverts for the *T-Touch* presently being shown in Italy are marvellously vivid and sharp. I'm no film buff, but I must say that the images, which almost flood on to the retina, often with no voice-over, and frequently with a discreet background score, are extremely appealing.

And now, ladies and gentlemen, the prize winners are …

On 7th November 1975, Tissot won a gold medal at the International Festival of Film and Television in New York for its advert «Kayak PR518», produced by Frama. In 1973, the film «Seastar Buggy» had won a silver medal at the same festival.

In 2001, Tissot captured two gongs – one at the «British POP Awards», and a «Popa Oma Outstanding Merchandising Achievement» award for the Tissot Vision Watch Display, featuring a video screen.

Do you keep up to date with the cinema?

Well, I do know the names of some major festivals, such as Cannes, Deauville, Avoriaz, Locarno and Berlin.
Talking of Cannes …

In Cannes, in June 2002, Mr. Nicolas Hayek received a prize at the International Advertising Festival. The TV presenter said that it was the «Advertiser of the Year» Award. She also said that, by awarding Mr. Hayek the Festival Lion, the jury had honoured him for his creative and innovative work. You know… the Swatch adverts.

Concerning the little masterpiece, he continues, *Do you want us to finish the evening with a quality short film?*

«Profile of the Future», directed in 1971 by a local film-maker, is an eloquent reportage on Tissot's highly specialised industrial activity, with all its skills and technological innovations. The camera wanders around the vast modern factory, through offices and packing and dispatching areas, through laboratories (ultrasound, galvanoplastics, injection of plastic materials), through the synthetic materials department, through workshops where *ébauches* and mechanical components are made, through assembly and reassembly workshops, and departments for setting, verifying and observing.

It's a tremendous film. Just think how quickly time passes, my neighbour sighs, conquered for an instant by nostalgia.

But things were already so modern! They even had a water purification plant for chemical plating!

The small private cinema is plunged into silence and shadows.

The session has come to an end. We adjust to the new atmosphere.

A virtual film continues to unwind in our heads.

I've been given three CDs.

«Tissot Carrousel... » warble «The Play Boys», an Asian group apparently specialising in out-dated rock music.

«Ceraten... Tissot... » replies a syrupy German singer.

«Two-Timer Tissot... » is the last refrain of an inaudible chorus accompanied by some choppy and fairly unappetising rhythms!

How quickly time passes, indeed, I smile to myself.

After all, don't they say that time flies?

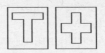

I t's pouring with rain and a storm is growling in the Valley of Le Locle. I increase my pace.

I have a *rendez-vous* with Tissot's technological history. I'm a little intimidated.

We have agreed that he is to tell me about manufacturing, the rationalisation of the factory, the adoption of the single calibre. He also suggests that he should give me a rundown on the company's contemporary technological wonders.

«He» is a former director of the *ébauches* department, a technician. He knows Tissot's history like the back of his hand.

Have you been told about what the établissage *department does, about its pocket watches and pendants? Let's see what happens in manufacturing.*

He gives me much accurate information in a short space of time. Of course, «accurate» is a word associated with Swiss watches.

In 1916, Tissot began to change its workong methods.

First, buildings were planned and qualified personnel hired.

Then, factory equipment was purchased – feet for the workbenches, pedals, pulleys, countershafts, coupling sleeves, and transmission shafts.

Technicians, *ébauche*-makers and technical directors got to work and built the first Tissot calibre.

Always on the lookout for new technical approaches...

My companion is in no doubt. The reasons behind this kind of organisation are clear – the system brings down the cost price, increases profit margins, and allows for more flexibility when it comes to dealing with market demand.

By 1920, all the components in Tissot watches were interchangeable. The most up-to-date mechanical machinery was used in production, and rigorous verification procedures guaranteed the system's efficiency.

More and more new Tissot calibres are created. Their catalogue is filled with different versions, different shapes, calibres for men and calibres for women. You've seen the anti-magnetic watches, the automatic ones, the calendars, small second hands, chronographs...

What a whirligig! But never a dull moment! In 1951, Edouard-Louis Tissot arrived on the scene.

A man walking down the street...
Advertising campaign, circa 1940.

While analysing the possibilities of a single calibre, Edouard-Louis Tissot noticed that the more calibres there were, the fewer of each of them could be produced. The manufacturer was thus reduced to making small series of similar pieces. In short, an economic heresy.

It was the beginning of standardisation.

The technicians calculate that between 1930 and 1960, Tissot produced 72 calibres. But this abundance of different models became a

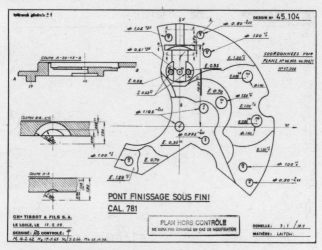

«Single calibre» production plan.
Tissot, Calibre 781, 1959.

thing of the past with the adoption of the «single calibre», with five possible finishes based on one *ébauche* – a watch with day and date, a watch with an alarm, an automatic watch, or a watch with other complications.

The chest of drawers is overflowing with different models.

It is a fine demonstration of the wealth of the company's collections, the variety of materials used, the technology applied and the designs chosen.

Visodate, Seastar, T 12... Stylist... Pinky... Carrousel...

In the Seventies, Tissot began to use original materials.

Tissot *T12*, circa 1960.

The «Sideral» line was introduced in 1969 and had a one-piece case in «fibreglass» and Swedish steel.

In 1976, the company introduced a quartz watch collection. The lifespan of their batteries was unequalled.

From the Tissot collection of the 1970s.

PR100, Rock-Watch, Pearl-Watch, Wood-Watch – «The Jewels of Nature» theme made its appearance in 1986. Then came *Ceraten* and, later, the *PR50*, the *PR200*, the *PRX*, the *Titanium*.

New ideas, new technological challenges. Cases in granite, mother-of-pearl or wood. An immediate success, which is repeated with a twin-display, LCD and analogue – the *Two Timer*, a watch you can trust.

The dial of the Tissot *Two-Timer*, 1984.

Madame has arrived.

I am one of the women who have adopted the latest Tissot models – the T-Collection, the Bellflower and the others have all seduced the ladies. It's a good thing that people are designing very feminine watches for us again, watches like charming jewels.

She is followed by her son.

Have you seen my T-Touch? It's great! All my mates want one … I can do all sorts of things with it. Look, I just touch the glass with my finger and I get hours, minutes (with hands), seconds (LCD display), date, weather, altimeter, chronograph, alarm and LCD display thermometer. And it's water-resistant too. The watch of the future … Innovation at your fingertips!

I am very familiar with the magic timepiece now.

تيسو TISSOT تقرأ 24 توقيتاًعالمياً بمجرد تحريك الإطار

دار تيسو السويسرية استعادت ساعة «نافيغيتور» Navigator المصممة عام 1953 وأخرجتها في حلة جديدة عصرية. وأهم ما في الساعة أنها تقرأ الوقت المحلي والوقت في (24) مدينة من مدن العالم أسماء (12) منها محفورة على إطار العلبة وأسماء (12) الأخرى داخل الميناء ويكفي تحريك الإطار إلى اسم المدينة المطلوبة حتى نعرف الوقت فيها.

حلة جديدة

Tissot in the Orient, 2002.

It's the perfect illustration of Tissot's century-and-a-half-old tradition of innovation...

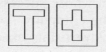

I t's early in the morning and the phone's ringing. It's Pius Felber inviting me to a Formula 3 race!

Put some proper shoes on and you can try the car! We'll provide the crash helmet...!, he jokes.

In fact, we had agreed to talk about motor sport sponsorship.

Talk is one thing, but actually getting into one of those machines is quite another!

Seated in a comfortable British car on our way to the track, the Tissot Vice-President explains the relationship between racing cars and the company's image.

Stage 1: the new version of the PR516 and its famous perforated bracelet just before the tumultuous events of May '68... 'PR' means «Particularly Robust». The initials are also a reference to the Precision of the watch.

We stop briefly by the lake shore to meet the designer of the second generation of the *PR516*, a model whose success is a legend in the annals of the company. A former creator-designer and advertising executive, he now dedicates his talents to painting. He has been warned of our arrival at the last minute via mobile phone. He does not hide his surprise at seeing us.

It was 1956. The brief was a simple one. A memorable advertising campaign was needed to ensure the success of the new automatic, anti-magnetic *PR516*, with its day and date calendar.

I found my inspiration during three visits to the premises of the company's suppliers:

– At a bracelet maker's in Geneva, my attention was caught by a strip of perforated metal. This metal strip gave me the idea for the perforated bracelet.

– During a visit to Ebauches Electronic, I stopped to look at a racing-car steering-wheel which had holes to hang stopwatches from. The link between the two ideas was obvious.

– Lastly, with the help of an advertising agency in Lausanne, I developed the link between image and product. The hand-on-the-wheel + PR516 with a perforated bracelet was born.

Tissot *PR 516*, 1965.

The resulting sales were tremendous, Mr. Felber confirms, to the embarrassment of the modest designer.

Let's say that Tissot was working on developing a modern brand image. In 1956, the international campaign based on the association of images that I had created targeted people who were 'young at heart', dynamic and active.

I must bring the following fact to your attention – the campaign derived its strength from its theme: a theme instantly recognisable in Hong Kong, Frankfurt, Buenos Aires and Wellington, New Zealand.

Before we go, he recounts a charming anecdote.

In 1968, a 15- year-old boy living in Thoune had saved up some pocket money to buy himself a Tissot PR516. He sent his piggy bank to the company offices with an accompanying note asking if there was enough money inside for the watch! Naturally, we took the opportunity of inviting him to Le Locle to choose a watch for himself!

Mr. Felber looks at his *T-Touch* and frowns.

Come on, quick … let's see what Formula 1, 2 and 3 racing is like!

Vroum… vrouuuum, vrouuummmmm.

We're off!

I have a small steering wheel with me. It is soft to the touch and at its centre is a large PR516 watch.

You'll have an original piece of decor for your desk! But, I am thinking, *Is it appropriate for a dyed-in-the-wool pedestrian like myself?*

We drive smoothly across the Swiss plateau. We can see the Alps cutting jagged shapes into the horizon. Eiger, Mönsch, Jungfrau…

There's traditional Swiss music on the car radio – so that's what those famous Berne yodellers sound like!

The rural serenade is interrupted by an announcement about a competition organised by Tissot and RTL. The prizes? Tickets for a race at the legendary Hockenheim track.

I am beginning to understand the reasons behind Tissot's sponsorship of today's event.

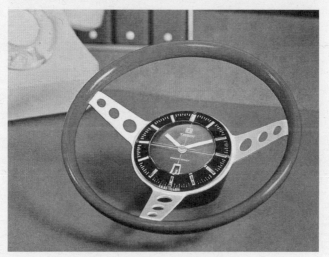

Tissot *PR516* at the wheel...

Can words alone describe it? The noise produced by the Formula 3 circuit is unbelievable. I can't even tell you the name of the place we've come to. I can't shout that loud!

Mr. Felber introduces me to the young driver, Tobias Blättler, who is wearing Tissot's colours.

I have been cheering for the red car with the Number 8 on it.

Performance by Tradition, Tissot 2002.

«Performance by tradition. Tissot». The banner cracks in the wind. The link between the four words is clear to me.

Isn't it just a single step from precision to the nearest millimetre to precision to a millionth of a second?

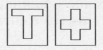

The taxi drops me off outside a shop in Le Locle, a shop faithful to the Tissot brand for several generations.

There are more surprises to come!, the driver tells me with a wink. Perhaps he has guessed that I am not an ordinary tourist.

The shop window curves around the corner of a typical 19th century building. There are stairs leading up to a dark façade; there is a ramp and a modest awning.

There is a blue sticker on the window on which is written: «Tissot, Lotus Formula 1»...

A vibrant chime of bells and the door opens.

The shop has a wide counter. Hanging from the walls I can see cuckoo clocks, modern timepieces made from plastic materials and Neuchâtel-style clocks with traditional painted patterns on varnished wood. There are also a few tin pieces amongst all this finery.

I notice a large individual working away at the back of the shop. It's probably the owner, busy repairing some humming bird or other. (A «humming bird» is a Neuchâtel term for a cheap watch.)

Looking around the room, I see a watchmaker-repairer diploma and a poster for the Le Locle section of the FTMH (the Metalworkers' and Watchmakers' Federation).

A photograph, but of what? A number of people strike a pose outside the shop. Judging by their clothes, I'd say that it was taken in the 1970s.

I hear a young man's voice.
How can I help you, sir?

He has a watchmaker's *migros* on his forehead. He must be the boss.

You seem to be interested in the photograph.

I nod in agreement.

It's a souvenir of the Lotus Formula 1 team's visit to Le Locle, organised by Tissot in September 1979. Some people still remember the welcome given to Colin Chapman at the little airport at Les Eplatures, where he posed at the wheel of his John Player Special. You can see my mother and father, both great Formula 1 fans, in the photo.

Tissot Lotus, 1979.

Now I understand what the taxi driver meant. My new acquaintance explains further.

A well as being a sponsor, Tissot was also the official timekeeper of the Lotus Formula 1 team, and of drivers like Mario Andretti, Carlos Reutmann and Mario De Angelis until 1982. The car featured the logo «Tissot Quartz», which referred to the multifunctional TS-X2 introduced in 1979 as part of the «F1» range.

As part of the sponsorship operation with Lotus, Tissot used to rent the legendary «Orient Express» to take over one hundred clients to the Hockenheim race track in style.

He disappears into his workshop for a moment.

He comes back with a copy of Tissot's French-language in-house journal, *Coup d'œil* (The Glance).

Tissot started sponsoring racing cars in 1974. This was just the beginning of the company's – our company's – activity in the field. Thanks to television and the press, Tissot's name was seen thousands of times all over the world. And do you know what the effect of all this was? Poor little retailers like me were forever out of stock!

He laughs a hearty laugh, while I cast my eye over the following passage from 1974:

Tissot has decided to take a more innovative approach to marketing. Henceforth, as well as advertising space in newspapers, magazines and on television, we will be active in the field of sport. In this area, we already sponsor the Suisse Romande Youth Cup football competition and organise the markers on many ski runs. This year we will also be sponsoring Renault rally cars and a Porsche Carrera in the Le Mans 24 Hours event.

He reminisces once more about his father. In 1976, the Tissot Sports Club, made up of members of the company's staff, organised a coach trip to the Italian Grand Prix at Monza to see Peterson beat Regazzoni.

Jacky Ickx, who drove the «Ensign» car with the Tissot markings, finished tenth, despite the encouragement of the good people of Le Locle!

Since then, Tissot has been busy sponsoring other sports. Since 1996, the society has been the exclusive timekeeper of all the world championships in cycling and ice-hockey. Sine 1999 and 2001 repectively the brand has been present also in the world championships of fencing and motorcycling. Rugby referees also sport the Tissot colours in England.

Tissot. Official Timekeeper.

Sponsorship and official time keeping contracts compliment each other in partnership with Swiss Timing, the official timekeeper of the Olympic Games. I am impressed by the list of activities. You only have to look at the programme of some 50 sporting events around the world in which the company was participating in 2002 – from the motocross competitions in the spring to the Asian Games in Octorber ... and , in charge of it all as head of sponsoring at Tissot there is an American national who is an ex-world champion in motorcycling trials...

The watchmaker of the Rue JeanRichard suggests that we continue our conversation at the local *brasserie*.

Did you know that the brewers of Neuchâtel are also worthy of interest!

The watchmaker recounts yet more stories concerning the people from Tissot.

But allow me, in this context, to invoke a concept dear to the watchmaking tradition «professional secrecy»!

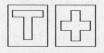

Today, I have taken the train to Bienne.

I have agreed to meet an exquisitely polite gentleman, whose immaculate calling card is embellished with elegant English calligraphy.

As the train moves smoothly through the Saint-Imier Valley (Saint-Imier, Villeret, Courtelary...), I note the company names which have recently become part of my baggage as an amateur historian of the industry – Longines, Cartier, Blancpain-Rayville...

Today's meeting is important, for it will enable me to form a clearer picture of the relationship between the Brandt and Tissot families. My curiosity has been piqued not only by the dials featuring the names of both Omega and Tissot, but also by the fact that Paul Tissot has been mentioned as Omega's Sales Director.

Naturally, I have done some research.

The company belonging to the brothers Louis Paul & Charles César Brandt, from Le Locle, originated as a watch shop founded in La Chaux-de-Fonds in 1848 by their father, Louis. Having moved to Bienne, the company created the Omega watch, rendered eternally famous by its visit to the moon.

We are sitting on a wooden bench in the Buffet de la Gare.

My elegant interviewee is the heir of those partners, who, in 1925, set up a production and sales deal which, in 1930, was transformed into a company.

I was a kid. Remember, I was born in 1916. But what do you want to know? I'm at your entire disposition, he says.

In a pure, formal French, he embarks upon his episodic tale.

The founding of the Société Suisse pour l'Industrie Horlogère [he spells out the acronym: S S I H] *is exemplary in several regards, not least because the project was undertaken during a recession.*

It was an original and complex association between two producers in the watchmaking sector.

The SSIH was from the beginning a financial holding company and a technical and commercial community of interests.

Omega, which had been weakened by its poor sales performance between 1920 and 1924, was looking for a partner to help it with its development. For their sales agent had broken his contract, while at the same time continuing to do business with all the company's clients. He had thus become, entirely legally, a direct competitor.

The Brandts reacted by hiring a new sales agent in the person of Paul Tissot, whose approach had impressed them.

The fact that Tissot's heir had taken on this project was in no manner disadvantageous to the Le Locle company, which, at the time, was actively looking for new markets for its products.

For the loss of the Russian market had the same nefarious effect on the two companies.

Survival was dependent on the tightening of the ties that bound them and the union of their respective strengths.

In effect, the aims and ambitions of the founders of the SSIH were compatible not only on the financial level, but also in terms of technology and production. Importantly, these shared interests were to lead to the development of a common approach to marketing.

The implementation of contemporary merchandising, advertising and marketing techniques – all of which were being developed apace – attested to a sophisticated understanding of the evolution of the watch industry and of its commercial needs. High-quality items were produced in large quantities at reasonable prices, while at the same time old concepts were updated.

The principal axis of the collaboration was the organisation of industrial production. First, the two companies respectively decided which calibres to retain and which to abandon, so as to avoid unnecessary competition with each other.

Secondly, the companies' directors developed agreements concerning both production and strictly technical aspects. Thus, the ébauches and components were made in Bienne for Tissot and the Brandt pieces were finished in Le Locle.

1930 thus marked the beginning of a new era for the Omega and Tissot watch companies. It provided them with a more solid base for their business and provided their customers with a more complete range of products.

For financial reasons, the companies chose to base their headquarters in Geneva, my companion confides.

What can I offer you? Are you hungry?

I am happy to accept. Without a pause, he continues his narrative.

In 1932, my father and my uncle supported a decision to purchase the Lemania company, founded by the Meylan family in La Vallée de Joux. A good company, which provided several calibres for Tissot and Omega.

From 1932 to 1951, the SSIH continued to expand, developing a shared production and marketing platform for its brands.

In the early summer of 1951, we learned the sad news of Paul Tissot's death. He had suffered a heart attack on his way back from Paris. We were stunned.

Paul Tissot (on the left), visiting his workshop,
in Le Locle.

He paints the portrait of a well-educated, sophisticated man, «aristocratic» in his bearing and his discretion. Paul represented the commercial side of the business. This led him to be somewhat distant from the «technical» side, despite the fact that he had a diploma from the Le Locle School of Horology.

He was a real character. There is even a portrait of him in Omega's boardroom; he's the only non-Brandt ever to have become a Managing Director of Omega. Professionally speaking, he was constant in his defence of SSIH's interests without ever taking an anti-Omega stance.

He smiles. *Do you think that his sister Marie was a little bit jealous of our relationship with her brother?*

Marie Tissot congratulates a an employee
of long standing, circa 1960.

She was the real boss of Tissot, she was a Tissot through and through and very possessive of Paul.

In 1953, Omega's directors initiated negotiations with a Bienne-based manufactory specialising in ladies' watches, which were sold under brands different from that of the mother company.

The SSIH holding company was an attractive proposition in the industry, so much so that the Bienne-based firm Marc Favre accepted a merger in 1955.

SSIH continued to purchase subsidiaries.

After Marc Favre, it was the turn of Rayville in 1961 and then Lanco in 1965. The Kottmann brothers of Langendorf both died suddenly within the space of six months. Negotiations were continued with their widows and their advisers.

Our parents made sure that the product ranges, choice of models and advertising campaigns were always coherent. There was also a certain amount of serious competition in the sector, with our two main brands both looking to gain ground in their quality-price categories.

The sommelier serves us a glass of cool white wine. Strangely, it has two labels: «Ligerz» in German, and «Gléresse» in French. *Don't forget that Bienne and its region are bilingual… Versteiht Der nid Schwyzerdütsch?*

Mr. Brandt concludes his long exposé.
Hours have passed.

Another word, however...

For a considerable time, the SSIH was basically a family concern. In 1966, over 90% of its capital was controlled by members of the immediate family. Then, with the difficulties caused by the crisis and increasing technological change, conflicts between the generations, were exacerbated.

Another word... He wants to underline the size of SSIH's retail network.

In theory, SSIH products were sold on a country-by-country basis through an independent general agent.
But life, my dear sir, as everyone knows, has little to do with theory.
And we prefer life to abstractions, even beautiful ones. So, these kinds of relationships were developed separately with each company which represented the brand, for, in effect, SSIH encourages the spirit of enterprise rather than the philosophy of the holding company.

The clock in the lobby strikes five. The fresco around it describes an allegory, «The Rondeau of the Hours».

The day has reached its end
And the hours have come full circle.
Day and night, aspiration and expiration.
Summer and winter, work and rest,
Wakefulness and sleep.
Such is the immutable law.

But I forgot to tell you about our industrialisation efforts abroad.

What is he alluding to?
I wanted to talk to you about a superb watch – a Swiss watch! – I was given. It was made in Mexico by Mexicans. The brand was Inresa, for which Luc Tissot was responsible and SSIH the umbrella organisation, and it was the tangible evidence of the success of an unusual project of the late 1960s.

He smiles.
Unfortunately, it did not adorn my wrist for long. As soon as my Managing Director saw the watch, he decided that, since he found it so aesthetically pleasing, he was going to keep it. I agreed to give it to him on the grounds that, from the public relations point of view, it would do the company more good if he wore the thing.

Another word about Tissot.
When I was in Le Locle, I got the chance to visit the Synthetic Materials Department. Edouard-Louis was very proud of it; he believed implicitly in the success of «his» plastic watch.

Between 1964 and 1971, the date of its launch at the Basel Fair, a plastic watch by the name of *Astrolon* (a name intended to bring to mind the word «nylon») was developed in the Tissot Research and Development Department. The department continued to

Tissot *Astrolon*, 1971.

fine-tune the product before launching it under the name of *Sytal* and *Idea 2001* (the latter was used only in the Italian market, the other moniker being *Tissot Research*).

I admit to never having seen such a watch, the description of which, besides its mechanical movement bears a certain analogy with the low-priced timepiece designed in Bienne.

Idea 2001, 1974.

The project got off the ground in 19562 with a patent for an 'oilless watch'. The project was named «Sytal» for «Système Tissot d'auto-lubrification».

He continues: *The Astrolon was ahead of its time, so far ahead, in fact, that it missed out on the most recent developments in the chemistry of plastics. Tissot's ultra-modern watch made a dramatic entry on to the market, but in fact it was already outmoded. We had used advanced materials to produce a watch whose basic technology was, well, four hundred years old! Consequently, electronic watches rapidly got the better of it!*

Just before leaving me on the station platform he says:

Images of the past stimulate and influence the way the people of Le Locle look at their town today.

I am happy that you are taking such an interest in the history of Tissot.

Sir, your own works of creation and memory assume the form of a beautiful Museum, which attests to the devotion of an industrialist to the watchmaking heritage of the city of Bienne. In Le Locle, the Tissot family works faithfully to promote respect for tradition, a tradition derived from the talents nurtured by the company since its foundation in 1853.

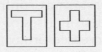

It will come as no surprise to you that I continue my research in order to prolong the interview which Mr. Brandt has granted me.

You will find the résumé of this interview below.

Despite certain isolated periods of stagnation, the Swiss watch industry grew steadily since the end of the Second World War. By 1975, while the economic crisis linked to the intense monetary upheavals of the time did its worst, people in the industry realised that the situation had changed. The Federal authorities were called upon to help. Support was forthcoming in the shape of economic development plans, tax breaks, aid for promotion and advertising, research in the fields of microelectronics and microtechnology, and unemployment insurance. As early as the end of the «watchmakers' holidays» in 1974, the situation was already showing signs of improvement, an improvement which was destined to continue. The SSIH, however, was confronted by world recession, the petrol crises of 1973 and 1975, the effects of increased protectionism, and the twin challenges of competition from Asia and the ever more important role played by electronics.

I am back in the company's headquarters, going through hundreds of press cuttings stored away in tightly packed boxes in the archives.

What is the common theme of these articles? Economic crisis! Everyone was worried.

I am joined by the archivist.

He comments laconically on the press cuttings laid out in front of us.

The closure of the ébauche *workshops, reduction in working hours and pay, lay-offs and rationalisation … Not a pretty picture.*

Ebauches destined for the rubbish heap, circa 1978.

The headlines reflect the situation: *Tissot to Cut Jobs on 1st October, Dramatic Times for Tissot.*

Tissot, which has been confronted with 'an awful situation' for the last five years and which has had to live increasingly within its declining means, has announced that it will cease manufacturing its own products in December 1977 and concentrate all its activities in Le Locle. Consequently, the branches at Peseux and La Chaux-de-Fonds will be closed.

While the SSIH is celebrating its fiftieth anniversary, the press seizes on a shocking piece of news. On 21st October 1980, they announce a loss for the enterprise of 42 million Swiss francs.

And when you think of the amount of time they spent trying to get the new company computer through the window! And the lift that gave way under its weight!

My interlocutor, who had himself been transferred to Bienne in 1971, and who came back to Le Locle in 1997, reminisces about «the catastrophe» with some bitterness.

After Tissot's senior executives were transferred to Bienne, there was a brief period of relative stability, relative, that is, compared to the preceding weeks of transfers and changes. The never-ending changes not only made relationships with salespeople and clients difficult (as we were isolated in Le Locle), but also, you know, adversely affected the relationships built up between individuals within the SSIH.

Some things are better forgotten. But time·is a great healer of painful memories.

However, thanks to the press, radio and television, everybody was aware of the situation.

In the watchmaking industry in particular, and notably at Tissot, times were tense and difficult. Everyone at every level had to work hard to ensure the survival of the company. In 1977, Tissot's directors decided to diversify, branching out into the field of medical instruments.

1981 will forever be associated with the débâcle *of the SSIH Group. But, please, don't let me keep you from your research.*

In 1983, everyone in Le Locle was under threat.

The thing that had had the whole town holding its breath for months was the possibility of a major rationalisation of the Fabriques d'Assortiments Réunis, a company affiliated to the ASUAG Group. It would not be long now before Hayek Engineering would deliver to ASUAG's directors in Bienne a plan to stabilise the delicate situation in which the company found itself.

Nicolas G. Hayek's final report makes several recommendations, including a merger between ASUAG and SSIH, which would become the SMH (the *Société Suisse de Microélectronique et d'Horlogerie*, or Swiss Microelectronics and Horology Company).

The merger is a success.
Tissot is saved!

WoodWatch, special series to mark the 700th anniversary
of the Swiss Confederation, 1991.

*It would, perhaps, be appropriate to bring to mind
the recent history of the Swatch Group.*

It is the early 1980s.

*On the one hand, there was the SSIH, which inclu-
ded the brands Omega, Tissot and Hamilton, as well
as an Omega watch manufactory. This last had seen
its reputation decline drastically. It was making
considerable losses and its directors were unable to
manage the fortunes of a major brand such as
Omega had been.*

On the other hand, there was the ASUAG, a holding company which controlled the production centres for ébauches, assortments and electronic components (…) and which supplied the entire watch industry.

The first step we took, all of us working together to create the present empire, was to show renewed respect for the brands, to care for them, and to produce them. In this regard, we had to conserve the heritage of the industry – unique to Switzerland – both in terms of quality and in terms of the number of factories (around a hundred). The jobs of 6,000 workers were at stake. [Message from President N.G. Hayek, Swatch Group Management Report, 2001, Bienne, 2002.]

I am anxious to get to the town of Bienne and visit the Swatch Group's headquarters.

My last few hours in Le Locle.

Outside the Town Hall, I take a last, lingering look at the beautiful fresco on the building's ample façade. Two wise astronomers armed with compasses divide up time, represented by the rays of the sun.

Men have divided the course of the sun, determined the hours …

Past Time, the Future, Abundance, Virtues and Vices, Arts and Crafts … Lace-makers of times gone by and watchmakers of today … Perseverance and faith, intuition and genius, fidelity and sincerity.

It is time to pack my suitcase.

As well as the lines I have committed to paper during the course of my stay, I am taking away with me a number of ideas upon which to meditate, formulae for the elaboration of a wise philosophy, lessons in life – and endless impressions.

I know that I have not exhausted the riches of the Neuchâtel region.

Past and future come together to give dynamism and innovation, and respect for tradition, a permanent foundation.

A car pulls up next to me. The driver's warm smile melts my serious thoughts away.

Get in, I'll drive you to Bienne. We can see the cyclists finish the last stage of the Tour de Suisse.

No sooner said than done! Here I am wearing a white shirt and a cap, sitting in a small but beautifully assembled Smart sports car.

The Smart is a little car which sprang from Mr. Hayek's fertile imagination, explains François Thiébaud. *His gift for invention helped him develop this revolutionary idea for a small, utilitarian vehicle. He designed a hybrid car, powered by solar energy and thus economical, a car especially good in traffic. Brilliant, isn't it?*

The wind pushes the little car along, a tiny point lost in the shadow of the imposing Chasseral.

Larger-than-life *Viatech*, Bienne, 1991.

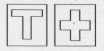

S watch Group, on the shores of Lake Bienne. The headquarters of the Swiss watch industry's future.

In the streets, Tissot banners are everywhere. For the Le Locle-based company is, along with the city council, sponsoring the last stage of the Tour de Suisse cycling race. Tissot is the event's official timekeeper.

François Thiébaud walks into the air-conditioned Swatch Group building in the Faubourg du Lac before me and is thus well placed to see my astonished reaction. He likes surprising me.

An immense Tissot *Navigator* watch attracts the attention of every visitor, an outsized instrument which gives the time in twelve cities on five continents. Every time zone is represented.

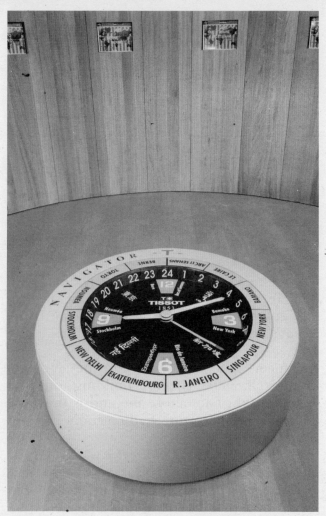

Navigator, Arc et Senans, 2001.

It was made in the year 2000 as part of an exhibition of the 'Ideal City' at the Royal Saltworks at Arc-en-Senans. The utopian structure built by the architect Ledoux, advocate of communal living, between 1775 and 1779 houses an irrational timepiece — and yet it is solid, a fine example of the traditional skills of the Jura.

A masterpiece.
We leave each other under the arch above the finish line … T I S S O T.
Goodbye!

The crowd applauds the Swiss winner. Well done, Alex!
I also learn, by chance, that Tissot is a sponsor of the new Olympic training centre at Aigle, at the gates of the Valais.

I close my notebook.

Once again, I am at the railway station.

I turn back the sleeve of my shirt to reveal the dial sitting prettily on my wrist, not to check on the punctuality of the federal train system, but to admire the gift offered to me by the participants of the public relations meeting to which I have been invited.

Tissot sports watch *V8*, 2002.

The new Tissot V8, featuring the logo of the Tour de Suisse 2002, sparkles with myriad virtual facets – those of my recently formed memories.

My collection of Tissot watches has been officially inaugurated.

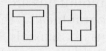

On the TGV that whisks me smoothly across the Jura countryside, I consult my watch.

A gesture of vanity? No, a gesture of thanks to those who have been so kind to me during my stay.

A break in the journey. A large banner on the station wall announces that the Museum of Time will open in June.

Past and future, philosophy of time and technology of time's measurement: the themes of my journey to the country of watchmaking echo in my mind.

The TGV eats into the journey. The dark green forests, the refreshing air, the cows, the horses and sheep – herds both sparse and numerous.

Between Doubs and the Crête du Jura, the Neuchâtel Mountains form the roof of the Swiss and French Jura range, beneath whose crenellated buttresses lie the Swiss lakes, the Vosges and Burgundy.

These gentle mountains are at the centre of everything. Geographically, they are equidistant from Paris, Brussels, Munich and Florence... Basel, Berne, Lausanne and Geneva are their neighbours.

Economically, they are in the maelstrom of technological expansion. Socially, they balance the opposing forces. Culturally, they have an intense existence.

Two towns.

Le Locle, «Mother Commune», City of Precision, over eight hundred years old.

La Chaux-de-Fonds, «Watchmaking Metropolis», veritable and typical industrial city of the 19th century.

One foot on the cultivated soil, the other in the workshop... and the emerald countryside all around.

Paris. The end of the journey.

Tired now, I return to the Hôtel next to the clock tower whose tall silhouette is broken into a thousand reflections by the glass façades of the buildings surrounding it.

The doorman nods to me before going about his business.

In the middle of the lobby – An exhibition on Time ... and Tissot is there yet again!

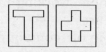

Another word, to complete these lines.

I might as well admit it, since I can tell that, for all my rhetorical artifice, you have already guessed who I am.
I am the narrator and signatory of this story.

I am the *confidante* of many authentic witnesses.
In revealing my identity, I confirm the veracity of this document.

In revealing my status as a lover of history, I attest to my penchant for stories – the stories told by great authors like Alexandre Dumas and André Castelot, as well as those recounted by Jurassian writers such as Madame Houriet, Alfred Chapuis, Armand Renner known as Labor, Achille Grospierre and many more.

Nothing is more enriching than getting in touch with history, through documents, objects and people: working in the present to prepare the future.

When such a trio of «components» is brought together, I can't wait to go through more library archives, find more fascinating people to interview, and to discover yet more primary sources. I shall return to the heart of the company to read yet other stories.

There is so much left to be read. Besides, haven't I already talked about how original the history of Tissot is?

Nothing is more interesting than participating in a vast project designed to conserve and validate watchmaking heritage.

Give a future to Tissot's past.

This is the motto that has linked Tissot's management and myself, a fortuitous union based on a shared interest in the aural history of Neuchâtel's watchmakers – our elders, our contemporaries and our young people.

Associated with the life of the company during several busy months, I have been able to appreciate the depth of this interest and the fact that it is destined to be rigorously prolonged into the future and to ensure the survival of authentic memories. An «active rather than a reactive» process, as the management would say.

Thank you for your Stoic perseverance and good luck to «La Tissot»!

And my thanks to all those I talked to, participants in Tissot's living memory and intimately involved in the elaboration of this narrative.

Estelle Fallet

Le Locle, 1st July 2002,
as Tissot enters its 150th year

For further information...

The Story of a Watch Factory,
is drawn from an extensive work of historical
research by the same author, Estelle Fallet,
published by Tissot in 2003 on the occasion
on its 150th anniversary and entitled:

Tissot, 150 years of history

This de luxe version is abundantly illustrated
and available in
French - German - English
Spanish - Italian

Price: 100.- Swiss Francs
(non including postage)

ORDER FORM

I should like to receive ..... copies of the

Tissot, 150 years of history

Chosen language:

French ☐   German ☐   English ☐   Spanish ☐   Italian ☐

SURNAME: ....

First name: ....

Adress: ....

Post Code, Country: ....

Nº .... - ....

e-mail: ....

Method of payment: Visa ☐   Mastercard ☐

☐☐☐☐ ☐☐☐☐ ☐☐☐☐ ☐☐☐☐

Control number   ☐☐☐
(verso)

American Express ☐

☐☐☐☐ ☐☐☐☐ ☐☐ ☐☐☐☐

Credit Card Expiry Date: ....

Unterschrift: ....

Please return your order form by fax or post to:
TISSOT SA
17, rue des Tourelles
CH-2400 Le Locle
Tel. + 41 32 933 31 11 – Fax + 41 32 933 33 11
tissot@tissot.ch – www.tissot.ch

© 2002, Tissot SA, Le Locle
A company of the Swatch Group, Switzerland.

ISBN 2-940333-02-5

Printed in 2016

Production by
Olivier Attinger,
CH 2067 Chaumont, Switzerland

Graphic design and blueprints by
Schmid and Muller,
CH 2054 Chézard Saint-Martin, Switzerland

Translation and rereading
Michael Lavin and Elisabeth Ingles

Original French edition translated into
English, German, Italian, Spanish, Portuguese, Polish,
Chinese, Russian, Persian, Arabic and Japanese.

Printed in China